HISTORIC LAKELAND

LONDON

IAN ALLAN LTD

Paul Canning

In loving memory of my
grandfather, Henry
Rickard Meyer

First published 1989

ISBN 0 7110 1771 9

All photographs © Paul
Canning 1989 except: Holker
Hall Staircase © Holker Hall
1989; Stott Park Bobbin Mill ©
English Heritage; Dove
Cottage, Grasmere, interior ©
Dove Cottage/The
Wordsworth Trust © 1989

All maps © Ian Allan Ltd, were
redrawn by Paul Bambrick
from originals supplied by
Alistair E. Paxton Baines,
BA(Hons), BArch (Hons),
Man.U.

Published by Ian Allan Ltd,
Shepperton, Surrey; and
printed by Ian Allan Printing
Ltd at their works at
Coombelands in Runnymede,
England

Contents

Introduction

The sanctuary of beautiful Lakeland has long enticed the many in search of the tranquility of this scenic mountain environment. People have been coming here since the mid-18th century. The Lake poets were drawn to this spot and found inspiration here, to compose such eloquent verse. Indeed, the great bard William Wordsworth was lured to Grasmere 'On nature's invitation'.

The Lake District is one of the most picturesque and unblemished areas in the country. It comprises high peaks (the highest mountain in England is here — Scafell Pike towers 3,205ft/977m above sea level) and smaller fells, upland streams, cascading gills and long rivers which snake a course down remote valleys; a wealth of tarns and 16 lakes (Windermere, Ullswater, Coniston, Bassenthwaite lake, Hawsewater, Thirlmere, Derwent Water, Wast Water, Crummock Water, Ennerdale Water, Esthwaite Water, Buttermere, Loweswater, Grasmere, Rydal Water and Elterwater). Twisting lanes lead to tiny secluded villages; cottages and farmhouses hug the fellside. Acres of moorland and 'a field or two of brighter green' are criss-crossed by dry stone walls; which wandering within these stone-bounded confines are the ubiquitous Herdwick and Swaledale sheep.

The Lake District was designated as a national park in 1951. It covers 880 square miles (2,279sq km) and is actually the largest national park in Great Britain. It is situated in the county of Cumbria in the northwest of England. Cumbria is a huge county — in fact the second largest in England — surpassed only by North Yorkshire, and covers an area of 2,629 square miles (6,809sq km). Before the 1974 reorganisation of local government and the ensuing boundary changes, Cumbria used to be split between the old counties of Westmorland and Cumberland. Today the new county, which extends as far as Carlisle with a population of about 485,000, is sub-divided into five districts: Copeland in the southwest, South Lakeland in the southeast, Eden in the northeast, Allerdale in the northwest and Carlisle in the far north. Around 70% of this land is used for agricultural purposes. The Lake District National Park boundaries extend from Cockermouth in the northwest, south to Cleator Moor and thence to Ravenglass on the west coast. From Cockermouth, heading northeast they spread across Allerdale District and then south to Penrith. From Penrith the boundary extends south to Kendal and thence to Arnside. From Arnside the boundary extends west to Broughton-in-Furness and thence to the west coast.

Today, many folk who sojourn to this beauty spot come to escape from the infernal din of life in the conurbations — 'to wander lonely as a cloud' — touring the fells, collecting their thoughts amidst serenity; but various outdoor attractions such as boating, horse-riding, water-skiing, angling, ornithology, cycling, fell running and rock climbing — to name but a few — are also reason enough to tempt visitors to the area.

Those in search of history and heritage visit the Lake District too. The layman and more informed historian alike journey from many a place to gain a knowledge of local heritage. Picture postcard ruined abbeys, castles and fortified dwellings shroud a turbulent past. There are fine churches (like the Norman sanctuary of St Michael's, Barton, and the smallest of them all, St Olaf's in Wasdale Head), stately homes, country farmhouses, ancient stone circles, the remains of Roman forts, restored mills and museums. They all tell us something of the types of life style followed by Lakeland man in years gone by.

To find out how the area was formed, one must first look at the geology of the landscape. The Lake District has three main rock types which give three contrasting types of landscape. In the north are the oldest rocks, the Skiddaw Slates which were formed some 500 million years ago from the build-up of layer upon layer of mud and clay deposits. The pressure exerted upon these layers caused the deposits to harden, creating the sedimentary soft rock known as shale. These rocks are structurally weak and have become eroded by 'freeze-thaw' (the action of water expanding and contracting inside the rock joints, causing flaky fragments to break off). This has resulted in the angular peaks of the northern Lake District, such as Skiddaw (3,055ft/931m). Heather covering is extensive in the lower areas. A period of explosive volcanic activity followed the Skiddaw Slates deposition resulting in the formation of very hard rocks with a strong resistance to erosion, which are known as Borrowdale Volcanics. These rocks form the characteristically craggy outline of peaks of the central Lake District, such as the Langdale Pikes and the Scafell Range. During the Silurian Period which occurred about 400 million years ago, the land was covered by sea which left layers or beds of silt deposits. The pressure on these deposits resulted in the formation of Silurian Slates. This type of rock is easily eroded and therefore forms more rounded, lower fells — those of southern Lakeland. It is also a rock which supports large expanses of greenery and woodland.

During the Ice Age, which occurred about two million years ago, there was a dramatic change in the climatic conditions. The ambient temperature nosedived: this resulted in a massive accumulation of snow and ice which helped to fuel the glaciers on their advance down from the north. These ice sheets, powerful tools of erosion, changed the appearance of the landscape — plucking out valley bottoms, creating more rounded U-shaped valleys, forming lakes and tarns, transporting debris from place to place and dumping it as morainic deposits. Post glaciation the erosion process continues, effecting gradual change in the landscape.

Mesolithic man first settled in the area around 5000 BC. He was a primitive hunter, employing crudely made flint stones for arrows. More advanced Neolithic settlers arrived in around 3500 BC. Neolithic man domesticated animals; he worked the land and reaped the benefits from crops planted for food. He scoured the Scafell and Langdale Peaks in search of hard volcanic rocks for stone arrows and axes. These tools were later precision finished, carefully cut to the right shape and used to fell woodland to make way for settlements. Late Neolithic/early Bronze Age man also possessed the means by which huge blocks of stone could be shifted from one place to another to build impressive stone circles, such as Castlerigg and Long Meg and Her Daughters. Bronze and Iron Age man continued in his sophistications: stone walls were built to define territories enclosing whole communities. For a long time settlers had journeyed across from Ireland to the west coast of England and from the east to this area, via the valley of Eden, and continued to do so for centuries.

In the first century AD the Romans invaded Britain. They were renowned not only for their incredible fighting abilities, but also as indefatigable builders of forts and

roads throughout the country. Hardknott Castle was one such example of a fort built (during Emperor Hadrian's reign, AD117-138) to accommodate 500 men. Its function was the patrolling of the road which ran from Glannoventa Fort at Ravenglass on the west coast to Galava Fort at Waterhead, Ambleside. Another road ran from Ambleside to Brocavum Fort at Brougham, Penrith, via High Street (Bretestrete) (the 2,717ft/828m peak). Further evidence of the Roman occupation can be found north of Carlisle at Hadrian's Wall, built in AD122 to keep back the Brigante tribes. These Roman remains can be seen today and stand as monuments to their skill in building and strategic planning.

Roman occupation continued until the early 5th century. In around the 7th century the Angles came down from Northumberland; they were agriculturalists, building their settlements in areas of high fertility such as the valley of Eden on the east side of Cumbria. Native Celts tended to settle on Cumbria's west side. (Cumbria is actually derived from the name for the Celtic people, Cymry.) By the latter stages of the 8th century, the Vikings had raided the east coast from Norway. The word, Thwaite — a common place name in Cumbria — is Norse for a clearing in a forest. The Norsemen also attacked from the west coast and from Scotland; they conquered and eventually settled here. As well as a legacy of Norse place names, these Vikings built stone crosses. The best example, surviving for some 1,000 years is the cross in Gosforth Churchyard (*West Cumbria, north of Ravenglass — see Gazetteer*). When the Romans invaded Scotland under Antoninus-Pius (AD138-161), this led to the building of the Antonine Wall between Forth and Clyde to keep back the Scots and little did they realise that this so called new frontier would have such inimical repercussions in the centuries to follow. The border between England and Scotland was frequently disputed: battles were commonplace and families on opposing sides were at enmity with one another. This inherent rancour was to continue until the 17th century and beyond. In 1603 King James I (formerly James VI of Scotland), determined to suppress this belligerence, ordered a mass execution of pillagers and other nefarious offenders.

Right:
Jim Dixon at the 'hand roughing' machine at Stott Park Bobbin Mill.

Far right:
The 7th Duke of Devonshire's room at Holker Hall.

As a direct response to this border conflict, pele towers (towers enveloped by a defensive stockade), castles and fortified dwellings were constructed all over Cumbria (right in the heart of border country). Many of these 12th, 13th and 14th century pele towers which can be seen today, formed the basis for later additions. The huge pele tower at Sizergh Castle was built in around 1350. At 60ft (18m) in height, it is one of the largest to survive. This impressive structure was later added to in Tudor and Elizabethan times. Levens Hall and Muncaster Castle are other examples of pele towers built in 1300 and 1325 (respectively) with later additions. Dalemain was built as a pele tower in the 12th century. The present Georgian building, finished in pink sandstone ashlar has completely engulfed the original pele. Brougham, the Clifford family castle and Kendal Castle, once home of Katherine Parr (sixth wife of Henry VIII), with evidence of moats, gatehouses and loopholes (slits to accommodate the archer's bow) show that these were clearly defensive (as well as residential) structures.

The majestic ruins of Furness Abbey, a huge sanctuary founded in 1123 for Savigny Monks (who later joined with the Cistercian order) is situated just north of Barrow. This fine church was subject to many a raid by Scottish marauders, and in 1322 the resident abbot was forced to pay ransom to Robert the Bruce in an effort to prevent the usurption of the abbey.

The Dissolution of the Monasteries was indeed a traumatic time for the church. Many sanctuaries were unroofed and left to fester, others were totally destroyed. Resident brethren were forced to leave and in some cases monks were incarcerated and executed for recusancy. The Furness monks relinquished their place of worship on 9 April 1537 and the abbey was subsequently passed to Henry VIII's minister, Thomas Cromwell.

In the little village of Cartmel, the enormous priory church of St Mary and St Michael escaped with relatively few scars. Although the church roof was dismantled, other buildings were little touched. George Preston, who built nearby Holker Hall in 1604, undertook restoration work at the priory in 1620.

Industries and local trades in Lakeland have been diverse. Mining (which can be traced back to Roman times) and quarrying brought in quite a sizeable remuneration. Towns like Keswick prospered on the wealth derived from extracting iron, copper and lead. Agriculture has long played an important part in the economy of the area. Before the arrival of railways and efficient transportation and communication links, the Lake District — as other upland areas — was virtually cut off from the larger towns and centres. This meant that small communities had to provide for themselves and so water powered corn mills, like Muncaster Mill, Little Salkeld Mill and Heron Mill were born to cater for the needs of localised populations. Sheep farming has for centuries provided not only mutton and lamb, but more importantly, wool. The wool and cloth trade was firmly established by Flemish weavers who made Kendal their home in the 14th century. Kendal, 'The Auld Grey Town', built up an international reputation for its green cloth; naturally, prosperity followed. By the mid-18th century Kendal was flourishing. Carlisle initially became the centre of the woollen trade until the giant textile mills in Lancashire and Yorkshire took over.

Bobbin Mills were built all over Cumbria in response to the huge demand created by the textile industry for wood bobbins, needed for holding twine, wire and thread. Stott Park Bobbin Mill built by John Harrison in 1835 is one such example. Sadly, the exponential increase in mechanisation took its toll on many of the traditional industries and local crafts. The invention of the plastic bobbin reel and the eventual contraction of the Lancashire and Yorkshire mills, forced many wood bobbin mills to close down. Likewise, when Britain started to import Canadian wheat, it made economic sense to build the corn mills at the ports. This saw the death throes of many a mill in the 1950s. Heavy industry (iron ore and steel, coal and shipping), which used to be centred around Whitehaven and Workington on Cumbria's west coast, has seriously declined. Today, these have been replaced by chemical industries.

The Lake poets, writers and painters sowed the seeds to popularise the area from the mid-18th century onwards (Wordsworth's Guide to the Lakes was published in 1810). As a result, an increasing number of people wanted to visit Lakeland. The introduction of railways in the mid-19th century, and 20th century road networks, have made this ever more possible. Today, tourism is the Lake District's primary industry. Many of the old mills have been renovated and are now.open as working museums. Likewise, a wealth of stately homes and other historic buildings, some of which were worked on by master architects (Paley and Austin, for example, built a new wing at Leighton Hall in 1870 and also the new west wing of Holker Hall from 1871-75; Anthony Salvin carried out restoration work to Muncaster Castle's octagonal library, in 1862) are open to the public, many of which have been restored to their former splendour. The Museum of Lakeland Life and Industry in Kendal comprises room sets and workshops which have been brilliantly reconstructed to show virtually every facet of Lakeland life and tell the visitor something about the social and economic progression of bygone Lakeland to the present day. Abbot Hall (across the courtyard from the Museum), a restored Georgian building, is today one of the north of England's top art galleries; all of the rooms on the ground floor contain typical period furniture. In the little village of Troutbeck southeast of Ambleside is Townend, a unique example of a 17th century statesman or yeoman farmer's dwelling. Townend is a living document of one type of family's existence (the Brownes) in the Lake District. Swarthmoor Hall, south of Ulverston, is famous for its close ties with the Quaker movement; Leighton Hall, lying just outside the National Park near Carnforth, is famous for its Gillow furniture collection and display of falconry. The birthplace of William Wordsworth can be seen in Main Street, Cockermouth. The great poet spent many happy childhood years in this huge Georgian residence, originally built for Joshua Lucock, Sheriff of Cumberland, in 1745. Dove Cottage in Grasmere, once an inn called *The Dove and Olive Bough*, was the Wordsworth family home from 1799-1808. Rydal Mount, situated between Ambleside and Grasmere, was the last home of William Wordsworth before his death in 1850.

The aim of this book is to whet the appetite of the visitor to Lakeland, outlining a history of some of the more obscure places of interest, such as Long Meg and Her Daughters stone circle and St Olaf's Church, Wasdale Head, as well as some of the more well known sites, such as Holker Hall and Furness Abbey. The large map on page 11 pinpoints all 28 sites in the Lake District, while the Gazetteer provides a form of cross-referencing.

Each of the outlined sites contains a small location map and information details which give the following details: grid reference, location, how to get to the site, address and telephone number (where applicable) of site, admission charge, opening times, facilities available, car parking, toilets, refreshments, address and telephone number of nearest tourist information office, and other sites of interest.

For details of what's on and where, details of local buses, hotels, guest houses etc, contact Tourist Information.

Far left:
The summer house at Rydal Mount seen from the far terrace.

Left:
Long Meg.

'How to get to the Lake District'

By Road: Southeast and southwest Lakeland (Kendal, Windermere, Coniston and beyond, Newby Bridge, Cartmel, Furness and West Cumbria) can be reached from Junction 36 of the M6 motorway.

By Rail: Travel to Oxenholme station (southeast of Kendal), on the main line from London Euston and change. The visitor can then take the branch line to Kendal and Windermere from here.

By Rail for the west coast: Grange-over-Sands, Cark and Cartmel, Ulverston, Barrow-in-Furness, Cumbria's west coast; stations to Ravenglass and north to Whitehaven, Workington and Carlisle can all be reached by changing at Carnforth station (also on the London Euston to Scotland main line).

By Road: Northeast and northwest Lakeland (Penrith, Ullswater, Keswick, Cockermouth) can be reached from Junction 40 of the M6 motorway.

By Rail: Penrith station (on the London Euston to Scotland main line).

The Lake District is associated with a wealth of famous names, past and present: Wordsworth, Coleridge, Southey, John Ruskin, Beatrix Potter, Fletcher Christian and John Dalton — and today A. Wainwright, Hunter Davies, Melvyn Bragg and Chris Bonnington — to name but a few.

I was first drawn to this delightful place during my schooldays and every time I return, not only are old memories of mountain club walks rekindled, but there are always new experiences for the mind to treasure. On one recent occasion I stood alone with my camera on the shores of Wastwater. It had been raining heavily, but the scene was clearing and as I watched the passage of sun behind several ominous, but broken clouds, I waited with tremulous excitement for it to emerge. Suddenly, light and shade played on the scene, the whole coming together like some incantation . . . it was then that I pressed the shutter. Awestruck, I knew that I had to return again soon.

We owe a great deal to the mid-18th century conservationists and to Wordsworth and his contemporaries who first realised the importance of land conservation. Indeed, when Mr English built the house named Belle Isle (on the island of the same name) on Lake Windermere, in 1774, it met with much criticism. It was seen as a blot on the landscape. Wordsworth called it a 'pepperpot', and so under Isabella and John Christian Curwen's ownership trees were planted to make the house more discreet in its surroundings. Today, among other duties, the Lake District Special Planning Board/ National Park Authority scrutinise any development proposals in the Lake District National Park which might otherwise be detrimental to the beauty of the area. Together with organisations like the National Trust and English Heritage (The Royal Commission on the Historic Monuments of England), they help preserve the many stately homes, castles, historic buildings and sites, park and woodland, for the benefit of ours and future generations.

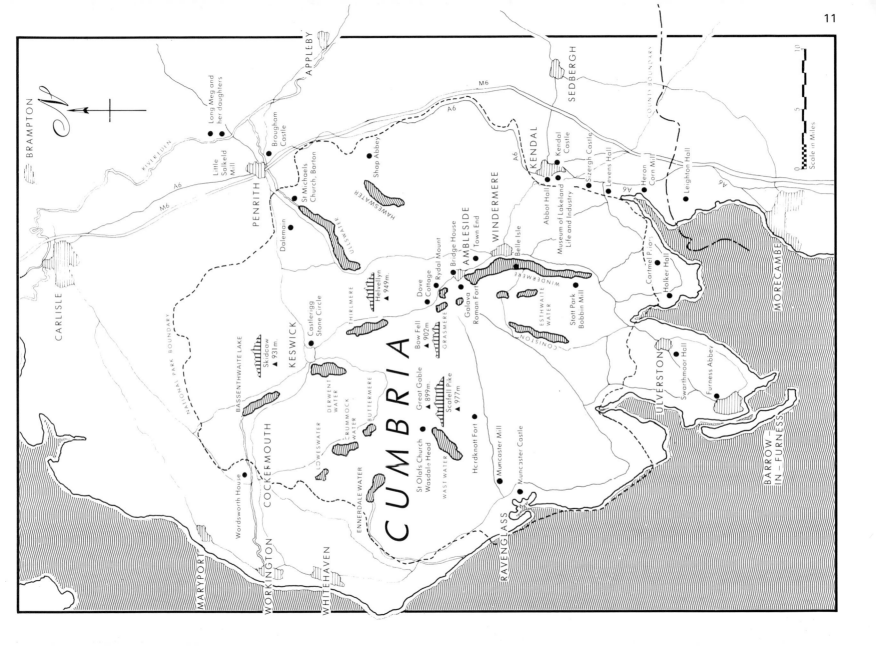

BRAMPTON

APPLEBY

N

Long Meg and
her daughters

Little
Salkeld Mill

Broughham
Castle

RIVER EDEN

CARLISLE

M6

A6

PENRITH

St Michaels
Church, Barton

Shap Abbey

M6

A6

SEDBERGH

KENDAL

Kendal
Castle

Abbot Hall
Museum of Lakeland
Life and Industry

Sizergh Castle

Levens Hall

Heron
Corn Mill

Leighton Hall

COUNTY BOUNDARY

A6

Dalemain

HAWESWATER

ULLSWATER

WINDERMERE

Helvellyn
▲ 949m.

Dove
Cottage
Rydal Mount

Bridge House
AMBLESIDE
Town End

Belle Isle

Cartmel Priory

Holker Hall

MORECAMBE

THIRLMERE

Castlerigg
Stone Circle

Skiddaw
▲ 931m.

KESWICK

BASSENTHWAITE LAKE

DERWENT
WATER

CRUMMOCK
WATER

LOWESWATER

BUTTERMERE

Bow Fell
▲ 902m

Great Gable
▲ 899m.

Scafell Pike
▲ 977m.

Galava
Roman Fort

GRASMERE

WINDERMERE

ESTHWAITE WATER

CONISTON

Stott Park
Bobbin Mill

ULVERSTON

Swarthmoor Hall

Furness Abbey

C U M B R I A

St Olafs Church
Wasdale Head

Herdknott Fort

WAST WATER

Muncaster Mill

Muncaster Castle

ENNERDALE WATER

Wordsworth House

COCKERMOUTH

MARYPORT

WORKINGTON

WHITEHAVEN

RAVENGLASS

BARROW -
IN - FURNESS

NATIONAL PARK BOUNDARY

10

5

0

Scale in Miles

Gazetteer

Abbot Hall   *OS Sheet 97, Ref: SD 517922*
☎ *(0539) 22464*

Abbot Hall is a restored Georgian residence, built in 1759 and situated in Kirkland, Kendal; it is next to the Museum of Lakeland Life and Industry and Holy Trinity Parish Church, on the bank of the River Kent. Abbot Hall houses one of the finest art galleries in the north of England. There are paintings by George Romney and John Ruskin together with displays and exhibitions. All rooms on the ground floor contain typical period furniture. *See p33.*

See also   ⋆ *The Museum of Lakeland Life and Industry, Kendal p36.*
⋆ *Kendal Castle p39.*

Appleby Castle   *OS Sheet 91, Ref: NY 685199*
☎ *(0930) 51402*

Overlooking the River Eden, the castle can be reached via the A66. The keep was built in 1176. A former home of the Viponts and the Cliffords, Appleby Castle was one of several fortified dwellings, restored by the great Clifford stalwart, Lady Anne, before her death at Brougham Castle in 1676.

Barton, St Michael's Church   *OS Sheet 90, Ref: NY 488264*

This Norman church, with chancel, nave and tower all dating from the mid-12th century, is situated a few miles southwest of Penrith. The most notable feature is the tower's double-rounded arch, believed to be Augustinian. Richard Wordsworth, the great Lakeland poet's grandfather, is buried in the chancel. *See p111.*

Belle Isle, Windermere   *OS Sheet 97, Ref: SD 393965*
☎ *(096 62) 3353/3360*

Built in 1774, this unique Georgian circular house stands on Belle Isle (island) in the middle of Lake Windermere. It has been the home of the Curwen Family since 1781. The rooms contain many examples of Gillow furniture. There are paintings by George Romney. *See p42.*

Brantwood, Coniston   *OS Sheet 97, Ref: SD 313959*
☎ *(0966) 41396*

The artist John Ruskin lived at Brantwood from 1872-1900. The house commands a fine view of Coniston Water. Brantwood contains many examples of the artist's work.

Bridge House, Ambleside   *OS Sheet 90, Ref: NY 376047*
National Trust Site

This tiny, two-room building which straddles Stock Beck (on the main A591) in Ambleside, dates back to the early 16th century. Since this time, it has been used as a tea room-cum-weaver's shop, an apple store, a summer house, a cobbler's and a dwelling. Since 1956 Bridge House has been an information centre run by the National Trust. *See p90.*

See also   ⋆ *Galava Roman Fort, Waterhead, p89.*

Brockhole, The Lake District National Park Visitor Centre   *OS Sheet 90, Ref: NY 389009*
☎ *(096 62) 6601*

Brockhole is situated on the A591 between Windermere and Ambleside. Opened to the public in 1969, it is a very good place to gain information about the Lake

District National Park, places to visit, what is on and where.

Brougham Castle   *OS Sheet 90, Ref: NY 536289*
English Heritage Site
☎ *(0768) 62488*

The ruins of this castle, once the home of the Clifford family, stand on the bank of the River Eamont, about a mile southeast of Penrith, and next to the site of the old Roman fort of Brocavum. The keep dates from the early 13th century. *See p115.*

Brougham: Countess Pillar   *OS Sheet 90,*
Ref: NY 548289
English Heritage Site

Situated about one mile east of Brougham Castle on the A66, Lady Anne Clifford erected this pillar when she parted from her mother in 1616.

Carlisle Castle   *OS Sheet 85, Ref: NY 397563*
English Heritage Site
☎ *(0228) 31777*

This large border defence dates from the late 11th century. The remains of the Norman keep, towers, rooms and passages may be seen. In 1568 Mary Queen of Scots was incarcerated here. The main gate (which dates from the 14th century) with its portcullis may also be seen.

Cartmel Priory   *OS Sheet 97, Ref: SD 380788*

The huge church of St Mary and St Michael, with its two diagonal towers, can be found in the village of Cartmel on the Cartmel Peninsula, which protrudes out into Morecambe Bay. This sanctuary was founded for the Augustinian (Black) Canons in 1188. After the Dissolution, it was restored in 1620 by George Preston of Holker Hall. The Priory is most noted for the oak screen in the choir, the carved misericords (c1440), and the enormous east window. In Cavendish Street, the gatehouse (built c1340) was the original entrance to the Priory. It has been the property of the National Trust since 1946. *See p52.*

Castlerigg Stone Circle   *OS Sheet 90, Ref: NY 293236*
National Trust Land/English Heritage Site

The circle consists of 38 stones dating from the late Neolithic/early Bronze Age (c1000BC) and may be found in a field about two miles from Keswick. *See p104.*

Dalemain   *OS Sheet 90, Ref: NY 478269*
☎ *(085 36) 450*

This Georgian building of pink sandstone ashlar was completed in about 1750; it began as a pele tower in the 12th century. The house is noted for (amongst other things) its Chinese Drawing Room, Fretwork Room of Tudor Fretwork Plaster and beautiful gardens; it is located just north of Pooley Bridge and a few miles southwest of Penrith. Dalemain has been the family home of the Hasells since 1689. *See p108.*

Dove Cottage, Grasmere   *OS Sheet 90,*
Ref: NY 343069
☎ *(09665) 544*

Dove Cottage, Grasmere, located north of Ambleside just off the main A591, used to be an inn called *The Dove and Olive Bough* and was then home of William Wordsworth and his family from 1799-1808. Many of Wordsworth's most famous poems — exemplified by 'Daffodils' and 'To The Cuckoo' — were composed during the years spent here. The rooms contain some of the original furniture. The Wordsworths landscaped the garden themselves. William Wordsworth and members of his family are buried in the graveyard of Grasmere's, St Oswald's Church. *See p97.*

Furness Abbey   *OS Sheet 96, Ref: SD 218717*
English Heritage Site
☎ *(0229) 23420*

The majestic red sandstone ruins of Furness Abbey, founded in 1123 for Savigny Monks, may be seen just over one mile north of Barrow-in-Furness. The walls of the choir, transepts and west (belfry) tower peak almost to their original height. The Abbey is also noted for its *piscina* and *sedilia* (in the Presbytery) and five beautiful arches with rounded heads as well as the remains of the Chapter House and other buildings. *See p64.*

Galava Roman Fort   *OS Sheet 90, Ref: NY 373034*
National Trust Site

The remains of this Roman fort, which date from around AD79, may be seen in a field next to Borrans Park at Waterhead, just south of Ambleside. The fort was built as one of several defences to control the road which ran from Glannoventa Fort at Ravenglass on the west coast, east to Hardknott Fort and then over Hardknott and Wrynose Passes to Little Langdale and thence to Galava. Among the remains are the Headquarters, the Commander's House and the Granaries. *See p89.*

See also ★*Bridge House, Ambleside, p90.*

Gosforth Cross   *OS Sheet 89, Ref: NY 072036*

North of Ravenglass (on Cumbria's west coast) and reached via the A595 (Barrow to Workington road) is the village of Gosforth, lying just east of the main road. In the churchyard (on the Gosforth to Wasdale road) is a well preserved Norse Viking cross. This slim and impressive structure, which stands some 14ft (4.25m) in height, dates from the 10th century. There are Norse, Pagan and Christian signs carved out of the sandstone, which tell of the power of good over evil.

Hardknott Fort (Mediobogdum)   *OS Sheet 90, Ref: NY 219015*
English Heritage Site

The impressive remains of this isolated fort, built during Hadrian's reign (AD117-138) to patrol the road which ran from Glannoventa on the west coast to Galava at Ambleside, may be seen nine miles northeast of Ravenglass. Among the remains are: the curtain wall, bases of towers, parade ground, headquarters, commander's house, granaries and an external bath house. There are superb views, not only from the fort, but also from the top of the pass. *See p81.*

Heron Corn Mill   *OS Sheet 97, Ref: SD 496799*
☎ (0524) 734858

This fully restored and working corn mill situated on the River Bela at Beetham, near Milnthorpe, dates from at least 1750. The visitor can see the milling process from start to finish. An exhibition which outlines its history is housed upstairs. *See p21.*

Hill Top   *OS Sheet 97, Ref: SD 370956*
National Trust Site
☎ (096 66) 269

Beatrix Potter (1865-1943) bought Hill Top in 1896. Many of her books were written in this 17th century farmhouse, which included characters like Peter Rabbit and Pigling Bland. The house can be found in Near Sawrey, which lies about two miles south of Hawkshead.

Holker Hall   *OS Sheet 97, Ref: SD 359774*
☎ (044 853) 328

Holker Hall, set in 22 acres of gardens and with a 120-acre deer park, is located west of Grange-over-Sands at Cark-in-Cartmel. The home of the Prestons, Lowthers and Cavendishs, the Hall was built in 1604 by George Preston. In March 1871 a fire gutted the west wing. The new wing, which can be seen today, was built for the 7th Duke of Devonshire by Paley & Austin. One of the many highlights is the oak cantilever staircase. *See p56.*

Hutton-In-The-Forest   *OS Sheet 90, Ref: NY 460358*
☎ 085 34 500

This is the home of Lord Inglewood; with its turrets, original pele tower (dating from the 14th century) and later additions, it is surrounded by beautiful woodland. It can be found about 5½ miles northwest of Penrith.

Kendal Castle   *OS Sheet 97, Ref: SD 522924*

The ruins of Kendal Castle which date back to the 12th century are perched on a hill, high above the 'Auld Grey Town'. The curtain wall, parts of four towers, the northeast wall of the great banqueting hall, one or two cellars and a large grassed-over moat, may be seen. Katherine Parr was born within these walls. She was later to become Henry VIII's sixth wife. The castle dairy can be seen in Wildman Street. *See p39.*

See also ★*Abbot Hall, Kendal, p33.*
★*The Museum of Lakeland Life and Industry, p36.*

Lanercost Priory OS Sheet 86. Ref: NY 556637
English Heritage Site
☎ *(06977) 3030*

Lanercost Priory was founded for the Augustinians in 1166. This quiet sanctuary which was the target for many a raid by Scots marauders in the 14th century is located northeast of Carlisle and Brampton, and just south of Lanercost. The nave was restored in 1740 and is still used as the parish church. However, the choir, transepts and other buildings are but mere shells.

Leighton Hall *OS Sheet 97, Ref: SD 498744*
☎ *(0524) 734474*

This white Gothic hall is situated north of Carnforth and just west of Yealand Conyers. Leighton is noted especially for the fine pieces of Gillow furniture — for example the 'daisy' table and early 19th century lady's workbox. Richard Gillow, the grandson of the founder of the furniture business based in Lancaster, bought the Hall in 1822. There is also a large collection of birds of prey. *See p18.*

Levens Hall *OS Sheet 97, Ref: SD 496851*
☎ *(05395) 60321*

Levens Hall — the home of the Redmans, the Bellinghams, the Grahmes and the Bagots — was originally a pele tower built in 1300 in response to the hostilities of border conflict. The Hall, situated on the bank of the River Kent south of Kendal, is renowned for its topiary garden, Elizabethan panelling, carved overmantels and steam collection. *See p25.*

Little Salkeld Mill *OS Sheet 90, Ref: NY 567360*
☎ *(076881) 523*

Little Salkeld Mill, northeast of Penrith, is a fully restored and operational corn mill which produces 100% wholewheat flour. The visitor can observe the milling process at close quarters, by appointment. *See p118.*

See also ★*Long Meg and Her Daughters, p120.*

Long Meg and Her Daughters *OS Sheet 91,*
Ref: NY 571373

The largest stone circle in Cumbria, Long Meg and Her Daughters (measuring 1,198ft/365m in circumference) can be found one mile north of Little Salkeld Mill. The stones, of which the tallest is Long Meg herself (standing some 18ft/5.5m in height) date from Neolithic times (c1500BC). *See p120.*

See also ★*Little Salkeld Mill, p118.*

Muncaster Castle *OS Sheet 96, Ref: SD 103964*
☎ *(065 77) 614*

Muncaster Castle, situated about one mile east of Ravenglass (on Cumbria's west coast) was originally an early 14th century pele tower. It has been the family home of the Penningtons for centuries. The many notable features of the castle include the octagonal library with tiny toy-like chairs perched on top of the Elizabethan table, the drawing room with barrel ceiling, Flemish tapestries and the Rhododendron and Azalea gardens. *See p68.*

See also ★*Muncaster Mill, p73.*

Muncaster Mill *OS Sheet 96, Ref: SD 096977*
☎ *(065 77) 232*

This restored corn mill, situated on the banks of the River Mite, can be found one mile north of Muncaster Castle whose records show that there was a mill here in 1455. The visitor has a chance to view the milling process and the associated machinery. The Ravenglass and Eskdale Railway passes the mill. *See p73.*

See also ★*Muncaster Castle, p68.*

The Museum of Lakeland Life and Industry
OS Sheet 97, Ref: SD 517922
☎ *(0539) 22464*

The Museum of Lakeland Life and Industry is close to Abbot Hall in Kirkland, Kendal, next to Holy Trinity parish church on the bank of the River Kent. It contains room sets and workshops, brilliantly reconstructed to show virtually every facet of Lakeland life. *See p36.*

See also ★*Abbot Hall, p33.*
  ★*Kendal Castle, p39.*

Rydal Mount   *OS Sheet 90, Ref: NY 364064*
☎ *(0966) 33002*

Rydal Mount, built in the mid-16th century, was the home of William Wordsworth from 1813 to 1850. The house contains many of the poet's belongings and the drawing room houses the only known painting of William's sister, Dorothy. Wordsworth landscaped the beautiful garden to his own designs: from the summer house at the top of the sloping terrace there is a superb view of Rydal Water. *See p93.*

See also   ★*Wordsworth House, Cockermouth, p101.*
★*Dove Cottage, Grasmere, p97.*

Shap Abbey   *OS Sheet 90, Ref: NY 548153*
English Heritage Site

The ruins of Shap Abbey, dedicated to St Mary, can be found on the bank of the River Lowther, 1½ miles west of Shap village on the A6. It was founded in 1180 for the White Canons. The early 16th century tower together with the remains of the east buildings can be seen. *See p123.*

Sizergh Castle   *OS Sheet 97, Ref: SD 498879*
National Trust Site
☎ *(05395) 60070*

Situated about three miles south of Kendal, Sizergh Castle has been the family home of the Stricklands for seven centuries. The magnificent pele tower dating from around 1350, together with Tudor and Elizabethan buildings, may be seen. The Castle is noted especially for the carved oak overmantels, oak furniture and panelling, Strickland family portraits and the rock gardens. *See p28.*

Stott Park Bobbin Mill   *OS Sheet 97, Ref: SD 373883*
English Heritage Site
☎ *(0448) 31087*

Stott Park Bobbin Mill, now a working museum, is located near Newby Bridge at the southern end of Lake Windermere and was built in 1835. It is an example of one of many such mills set up as a direct response to the huge demand created by the Lancashire textile industry for wood bobbins. The visitor can follow the bobbins through their various stages of manufacture on a guided tour with the mill's technicians. *See p48.*

Swarthmoor Hall   *OS Sheet 96, Ref: SD 282773*
☎ *(0229) 53204*

This Elizabethan Hall was built in 1586 and is famous for its strong Quaker connections. In 1652 George Fox, founder of The Religious Society of Friends (The Quakers), first came to Swarthmoor to preach. The Hall is noted for its carved oak panelling and newel staircase. *See p61.*

Townend (Troutbeck)   *OS Sheet 90, Ref: NY 407026*
National Trust Site
☎ *(096 63) 32628*

Southeast of Ambleside, in Troutbeck, is Townend, family home of the Brownes for more than four centuries from 1525 to 1943. The house, with its four large round chimneys, is noted for its carved oak pieces of furniture, crafted by members of the Browne family. *See p85.*

Wasdale Head, St Olaf's Church   *OS Sheet 89, Ref: NY 188087*

This tiny church is reputed to be one of the smallest in the country. It is situated in the hamlet of Wasdale Head, just to the northeast of Wastwater. Kirk Fell and Great Gable tower above, dwarfing this little sanctuary. *See p78.*

Wordsworth House (Cockermouth)   *OS Sheet 89, Ref: NY 118301*
National Trust Site
☎ *(0900) 824805*

This Georgian house on Main Street in the centre of Cockermouth, northwest Cumbria, was the birthplace of that great Lakeland bard, William Wordsworth, in 1770. At the back of the house, built in 1745, is the River Derwent. *See p101.*

Wythop Mill, Embleton   *OS Sheet 89, Ref: NY 178296*
☎ *(059 681) 394*

This restored mid-19th century sawmill can be found to the west of Bassenthwaite Lake and just to the east of Cockermouth, in the northwest of Cumbria.

Southeast Lakeland

Leighton Hall

Leighton Hall is the family home of Mr and Mrs Richard Gillow Reynolds and is without a doubt one of the best-situated in the country. About four miles from Carnforth, off the A6, close to the hamlet of Yealand Conyers, the visitor will emerge from twisting lanes to enter the grounds and catch a first glimpse of the white, Gothic limestone frontispiece at the far end of the huge park, with the Furness Fells in the background.

The history of the area dates from 1173 when William de Lancaster, the then Baron of Kendal, granted land to one Adam D'Avranches. Records show that D'Avranches had a fortified dwelling here in 1246.

The course of more than 800 years has seen 26 owners and only on two occasions has the ownership of the property been passed by sale. In 1786 Alexander Worswick purchased the estate. A Lancaster banker by profession, he was also the son of Alice Gillow. It was Worswick's decision to alter the appearance of the exterior from Georgian to Gothic style, after George Townley of Townley Hall had previously rebuilt the Hall in Adam style, 23 years earlier, on the site of an older house. In 1870 a new wing was built by Lancaster architects Paley and Austin, which houses the music room on the ground floor.

The Gillow furniture connection with Leighton was formed in 1822 when Richard Gillow (grandson of the founder of the furniture business) acquired the property. As one might expect, the Hall contains fine examples of the Gillow family's consummate skill in furniture making. In the dining room is an expanding table, chairs and a wine chest. In the hall, at the bottom of the staircase, is the 'daisy table' of eight wings. In the drawing room can be found an early 18th century games table and a lady's workbox, made for Mrs Richard Gillow in 1820.

Amongst other interesting features, in the drawing room on a French desk near a window are some buttons with a lock of James II's hair set in gold, which are kept in a case; the studio is filled with a collection of paintings by the late Mrs J. R. Reynolds. The staircase itself is magnificent: on its wall, among others, is the head of a Wapiti, shot in Canada towards the close of the 19th century. (The Wapiti was once the largest deer in the world.) Kathleen Ferrier gave one of her last performances in the music room here.

Leighton Hall is truly a delightful location and has been the setting for an episode of the well received 'Sherlock Holmes' television series, as well as featuring in the holiday programme 'Wish You Were Here'. It is also the home of the north of England's largest collection of birds of prey. Weather permitting, these birds are flown every summer afternoon and volunteers from a large audience on the front lawn get to put on the gauntlet and actually hold the birds.

The excitement of handling a bird of prey for the first time is but one of many attractions which all add up to make a visit to Leighton Hall an unforgettable experience.

Far left:
The Hall, showing Gothic-style pillars and front entrance.

Below left:
Lady's workbox (early 19th Century), by Gillow.

Below:
Staircase.

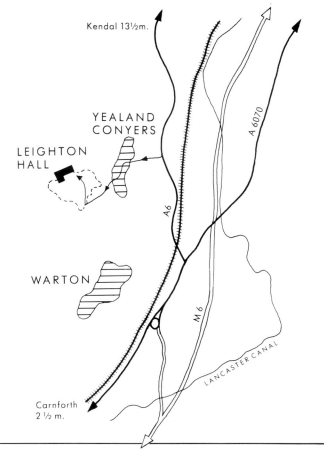

Above right:
The principal bedroom, of late Victorian style, was the bridal suite of Mr Reynold's grandparents.

Above Far right:
One of the many birds of prey at Leighton is the Pallas Sea Eagle.

Further information

Leighton Hall   *OS Sheet 97, Ref SD 498744*
Hall and ground. Afternoon display with birds of prey

Enquiries   Leighton Hall, Carnforth, Lancs LA5 9ST
☎ (0524) 734474

Location   About 3½ miles north of M6 Junction 35

How to get there   From M6 Junction 35, A6 north to Yealand Conyers. Turn off A6 and follow signs to the Hall, through Yealand Conyers

Admission charged

Opening times   May-September 2pm-5pm Tuesday, Wednesday, Thursday, Friday, Sunday and Bank Holiday Mondays. *(Closed: Saturdays, Mondays)*

Facilities   🚗; **WC** ; home-made snacks in the tea rooms; gift shop

Heron Corn Mill, Beetham
(near Milnthorpe, Lancs)

This corn mill — skilfully restored under the guidance of the Beetham Trust with its machinery in full working order — takes its name from a heronry which once existed on this site. It can be found between Lancaster and Kendal on the A6 about one mile south of Milnthorpe at Beetham. There are actually two mills in close proximity: one is concerned with the production of paper and the other, Heron Mill — reputed to be one of the finest in the northwest of England — concentrates on the milling of grain. Although the mill which can be seen today dates from around 1750, there may well have been a mill on this site for more than 750 years. Indeed, lands were given to the Coningshead Canons by the Lord of nearby Haverbrack Manor (Haverbrack is an area immediately northwest of the mill). Sir William Thorneburghe took over the lands when Coningshead Priory was wiped off the map during the Dissolution.

A natural waterfall on the River Bela provides enough fall to drive the 14ft-diameter wheel — the water being captured in its 40 iron buckets. The waterwheel itself dates from about the mid-19th century and is constructed of wood and iron. The power generated by the waterfall is used to drive no fewer than four pairs of stones. As late as 1930, Heron Mill, under the ownership of W. and J. Pye, was producing around 80-90 tons of corn every week.

The visitor can observe the milling process right from the initial stages of kiln drying of the grain to its travel down hoppers to the shelling stones (which effectively remove the husks from the grain). From here the grain progresses to the dusting machine which continues the de-husking process, to the winnowing machine (where a fan blows the residual pieces of husk away and also cleans the de-husked grain or 'groats', ie the kernels) and finally to the grinding stones where the grain is turned to flour.

On the ground floor is the driving machinery which, by means of gearing and shafts, connects the waterwheel to the main gearing which drives the four pairs of

Other places of interest
- ★Heron Corn Mill (see p21), 4½ miles north, on A6 at Beetham, near Milnthorpe
- ★Levens Hall (see p25), 7½ miles north on A6, via Milnthorpe
- ★Sizergh Castle (see p28), 9½ miles north, via Levens

 Town Hall, Highgate, Kendal, Cumbria
☎ (0539) 25758

millstones on the floor above. On the first floor is a large timber structure, known as the hurst (which was designed and put into place during rebuilding of the mill in 1740) which encloses the four pairs of stones and main drive gearing.

Due to the often unfavourable climatic conditions, mills situated in upland areas needed a kiln to dry the oats. After threshing, the grain would be brought into the kiln and spread over the clay-tiled floor. Heat from the fire beneath would then rise up and over a steel plate (a baffle), the function of which was to effectively spread the heat so that it would rise evenly through the multitude of tiny holes in the clay tiles. During this drying process, the grain would be shovelled over and over to ensure even drying. Hoppers placed each side of the entrance to the kiln provided a convenient receptacle into which the kiln-dried grain could be swept. From these hoppers the grain could be stored in bags and taken to the upper floor, via the sack hoist, ready for grinding by the millstones.

The original generator, which was in place in 1916, together with a generator dating from 1911 which was used in a Loughborough mill, are on show. The generator currently being used came from Witherslack Mill.

Stoneground products may be bought from the shop. The upper floor of the mill houses an exhibition which outlines the history of the place and the milling process. A tour of Heron Mill gives us an idea of what it was like inside a corn mill in its heyday.

Far left:
Heron Corn Mill.

Centre left:
This wooden hurst frame encloses the machinery used to drive the four pairs of millstones.

Left:
The Kiln.

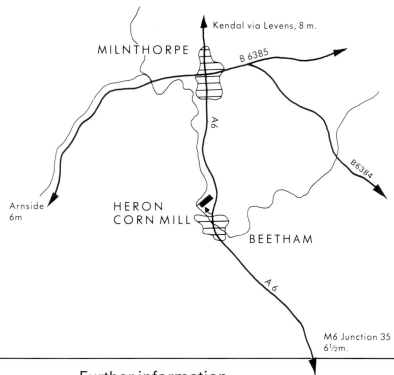

Further information

Heron Corn Mill *OS Sheet 97, Ref SD 496799*
The Beetham Trust

Enquiries	Heron Corn Mill, by Waterhouse Mills, Beetham, Milnthorpe, Cumbria LA7 7AR ☎ (0524) 734858
Location	7 miles north of Carnforth, about one mile south of Milnthorpe on the A6, by the River Bela
How to get there	From M6 Junction 35 (Carnforth exit), follow A6 north to Beetham

Admission charged

Above right:
Drive cogs and gearing on the ground floor which connect the waterwheel with the main gearing on the first floor which, in turn, drives the four pairs of stones.

Far right:
Don Ainslie, resident curator, operating the sack hoist.

Opening times	April-September, Tuesday-Sunday 11am-5pm
Facilities	🚗; **WC** ; refreshments in Milnthorpe
Other places of interest	★Leighton Hall *(see p18)*, 4½ miles south, via A6 and Yealand Conyers ★Levens Hall *(see p25)*, 3 miles north, via A6 ★Sizergh Castle *(see p28)*, 5 miles north, via A6 ★Kendal: Abbot Hall *(see p33)*, The Museum of Lakeland Life and Industry *(see p36)*, Kendal Castle *(see p39)*, 8 miles north via A6

 Town Hall, Highgate, Kendal, Cumbria ☎ (0539) 25758

Levens Hall

Levens Hall, renowned for its topiary garden, predominantly Elizabethan interior, steam collection and ghostly sightings, was originally a pele tower built in 1300 in response to the traumas of border conflict.

From about 1170 when the Baron of Kendal, William de Lancaster, granted a charter to Norman de Redman (whose surname was formerly de Hieland), enabling the first family here to build their pele and adjoining hall during the latter half of the 13th century; to the present day, only twice has ownership of this splendid mansion been passed by sale.

The first occasion was in 1562 when the 15th and last de Redman to own Levens, Mathew VI, sold the property to his cousin, Alan Bellingham. Alan died six years later, leaving the property to his son, James. James Bellingham, later to be knighted by King James I, set about a truly remarkable transformation of the Hall in Elizabethan style, panelling the rooms in oak and plastering the ceilings in around 1580.

Levens Hall was sold for the second time in 1686, when the last of the Bellingham owners, another Alan, reportedly lost the whole estate through gambling and was forced to hand over the Hall to the trustees. Alan's cousin, Col James Grahme purchased the estate from the trustees for the grand sum of £24,000 in 1688. The Colonel built the south wing to accommodate offices, brewhouse and servants' quarters. In 1692 Col Grahme brought in the much sought-after designer, Monsieur Beaumont, to lay out the magnificent topiary gardens which have remained unchanged ever since. Beaumont also worked on Hampton Court gardens in Surrey. This fact is mentioned on his portrait, which hangs in the great hall.

The last descendant of the Colonel was Mary Howard, the daughter of Frances (née Howard) and Richard Bagot, and it is from this line that the present family owners, the Bagots, are descended.

The great hall reflects James Bellingham's liking for Elizabethan panelling. He has complemented this with an impressive plaster ceiling. He also panelled and

plastered the drawing room in the same style. A pair of Sir James Bellingham's pistols, dated 1601, may be found in the hall. The drawing room furniture is of superior quality, dating from the reign of Charles II, but the most notable feature of this room is the 1595 overmantel. Another splendid overmantel, again carved of rich oak, is found in the small drawing room and features the Bellingham arms, with carved figures which portray the four seasons, the five senses and the four elements.

In the dining room the walls of Cordova leather are remarkably well preserved (the work of the Colonel in

1692). The Charles II chairs are reputed to be the best of their kind in the country. The upstairs bedrooms contain Indian Chintz patchwork. Quality furniture is the work of the famous Lancaster-based company, Gillow.

The Bagot family residence is also home to 'Little Gem', a half-sized tractor engine, one of a collection kept in the old Brewhouse, which illustrates a century's development of industrial steam power from 1820-1920.

The fine interior with its decor, Rubens paintings, furniture and Beaumont's éclat, the topiary garden, plus the steam collection combine to make a trip to Levens most worthwhile.

Further information

Levens Hall   *OS Sheet 97, Ref SD 496851*
House and topiary gardens; steam collection

Enquiries	Levens Hall, Kendal, Cumbria LA8 0PD ☎ (05395) 60321
Location	5 miles south of Kendal on the A6, north of Milnthorpe
How to get there	From M6 Junction 36, A591 and A6 exit, signs to Milnthorpe and Levens

Admission charged

Opening times	Easter Sunday-30 September Sunday-Thursday 11am-5pm
Facilities	🚌; 🚗; **WC** ; café and gift shop; picnic areas

Far left:
Levens Hall.

Centre left:
Elizabethan panelling and walnut and cane 17th century chairs (Daniel Marot style) in the bay window area of the large drawing room.

Left:
The richly carved overmantel in the small drawing room portrays the five senses, the four elements and the seasons of the year.

Above:
The library.

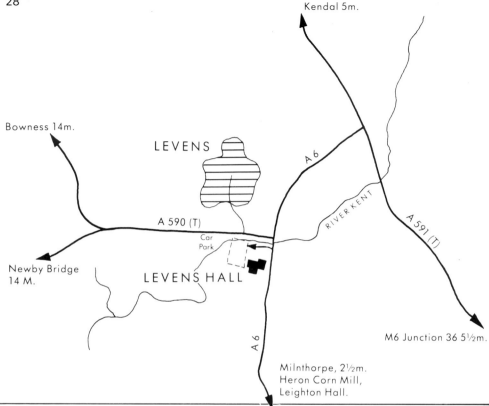

Kendal 5m.

Bowness 14m.

LEVENS

A6

A 590 (T)

RIVER KENT

A 591 (T)

Newby Bridge 14 M.

Car Park

LEVENS HALL

A6

M6 Junction 36 5½m.

Milnthorpe, 2½m.
Heron Corn Mill,
Leighton Hall.

Other places of interest

★Sizergh Castle (see p28), about 2 miles north
★Heron Mill (see p21), 3 miles south on A6 at Beetham
★Leighton Hall (see p18), 7½ miles south, via Milnthorpe on A6
★Kendal: Abbot Hall (see p33), The Museum of Lakeland Life and Industry (see p36), Kendal Castle (see p39), 5 miles north via A591 and A6

 Town Hall, Highgate, Kendal, Cumbria
☎ (0539) 25758

Sizergh Castle

Sizergh Castle, the family home of the Stricklands for seven centuries, lies just three miles south of Kendal. Henry II granted the Sizergh lands to Gervase Deincourt c1170-80. In 1239 the Deincourt heiress (Gervase's great granddaughter) married Sir William Strickland, whose family name was formerly 'de Castle Carrock' of Norman descent. From 1258 right up until the end of the 17th century, countless generations of Stricklands represented their county in Parliament. Joan, Sir William Strickland's only daughter married one — Robert de Wessington from Warton in Lancashire in the early 14th century. The first president of the USA, George Washington is descended from this marriage. In 1415 another Strickland, Sir Thomas, fought at Agincourt and later in 1448, in The Wars of The Roses; the family fought for the House of York. Sir Thomas's grandson — also called Sir Thomas — married Agnes Parr, the aunt of Katherine Parr who was later to become Henry VIII's sixth wife. In 1643, the great-great-great grandson of Sir Thomas Strickland and Agnes Parr, Sir Robert Strickland, was punished for his sympathies towards the Royalist cause and some of the Sizergh lands were sequestrated. Sir Robert's son, Sir Thomas, was also a passionate supporter of the Royalist cause and in 1688 he went into exile with James II, after the latter's abdication. In 1779 Jarrard Strickland married Cecilia Townley and in 1896 their great-grandson, Sir Gerald Strickland GCMG came to possess Sizergh. In 1931 Sir Gerald gave the castle to his daughter, Mary, who married Henry Hornyold (Mr Hornyold assumed the Strickland arms and name in 1932). Together with their son, the late Lt Cdr Thomas Hornyold-Strickland, they gave the Sizergh estate to the National Trust in 1950.

Sizergh Castle is dominated by the huge pele tower (with its dressing of Boston Ivy), the oldest feature, which was built c1350 during the turbulent years of border conflict. The original structure, enveloped by a defensive stockade, offered protection from the marauding Scots. This incessant enmity which lasted for more than two

Below:
Sizergh Castle.

Right:
Dated 1558, the oak screen in the entrance hall bears the family arms.

Centre right:
Tudor fireplace in the hall.

Far right:
Built in about 1350, the pele tower is one of the oldest parts of the castle.

Below:
This two-handed sword is a c1540 replica of an Edward III model (c1350) and can be found on the second floor of the pele tower.

centuries, until the Union of England and Scotland, was the result of the constant disputing of where the border between the two countries lay. Many of these peles were built during the hostile 14th-17th centuries. At 60ft in height and with walls more than 7ft in thickness, this pele at Sizergh is one of the largest to survive. A great hall dating from 1450 was built on to the pele on its northeast side in Tudor style. The hall was restructured in Elizabethan times and raised to the first floor, which gave

a larger area. Today, when the visitor enters the Castle he/she is standing in the old Tudor hall. A south wing was built in the mid-1500s. At ground level the various rooms were used as workshops. The huge room above called the 'barracks' housed the male servants' quarters. Building of the north wing commenced in 1565 under the initial direction of Walter Strickland (Sir Thomas Strickland and Agnes Parr's great-grandson). The kitchen was in use until 1890.

In the southwest corner of the Elizabethan entrance hall is a huge Tudor fireplace, an original feature. There is also a large refectory table finished in oak. The great hall on the first floor, of Elizabethan design and later reconstructed in the 18th century, houses some fine Strickland portraits. The large banner from the balcony above is that of Lord Gerald Strickland GCMG; before his death the banner was kept in St Paul's Cathedral. The transfer to Sizergh Castle was undertaken posthumously. The hall contains some Chippendale-style chairs of mahogany, crafted by Gillow of Lancaster. The Elizabethan dining room has been panelled top to bottom in oak. The ornately carved overmantel set above a Tudor stone fireplace shows the date to be 1564. The portraits include Charles II, James II and the latter's son, Prince James, better known as the 'Old Pretender'. Chairs in the dining room are of a different design with some finished in mahogany and others crafted in walnut. The decor in the Queen's Room (so called because of its overmantel which has Queen Elizabeth I's arms carved in it) is oak. Among the furniture is a Queen Anne *escritoire*, finished in walnut. The drawing room has been restructured over the centuries; among the contents is a collection of English pottery and china dating from the late 18th century and a corner chair, finished in walnut, of the 18th century. At the east corner is an Elizabethan gable. On the first floor of this block is the stone parlour (its name is derived from the room's stone floor which is patterned in black and white diamonds) which is typically panelled in oak. Marble facing of the fireplace was undertaken in around 1800. The linenfold panel room (linenfold panelling has lozenge-type shapes set into long panelling) is a small room-cum-passage which gives access to the rest of the first floor of the north wing. A

most interesting feature is the panelling, oak linenfold — the oldest of its design at Sizergh. It is reputed to date from the reign of Henry VIII. On the second floor of this east corner gable block are two small bedrooms, panelled in oak and both noted for their carved overmantels.

The second floor of the pele tower, noted for its adze-hewn floor, housed the family's private quarters. The window which looks on to the courtyard is 15th century. The refectory table dates from James I. The 17th century tapestry is Flemish. The two-handed sword, which hangs on the wall dates from c1540 (an Edward III replica) and is interesting because its dating coincides with the building of the pele itself around 1350. The top floor of the pele tower with its original 14th century windows and fireplaces and reached via the stone newel staircase, today houses a collection of Strickland valuables, including early deeds to the estate. There is also a showcase of costumes which date from the 18th century.

The terraced gardens date from the latter half of the 18th century. The lake may have been formed from a portion of the moat which encompassed the pele tower. Lady Strickland constructed the limestone rock-garden in 1926, planting a variety of different conifers. Sizergh Castle is set amidst some 1,500 acres of beautiful garden and parkland.

Further information

Sizergh Castle   *OS Sheet 97, Ref SD 498879*
National Trust Site
House, gardens and rock gardens

Enquiries	Sizergh Castle, near Kendal, Cumbria LA8 8AE ☎ (05395) 60070
Location	3 miles south of Kendal
How to get there	From M6 Junction 36, A591 to A590 interchange. Sizergh Castle is signposted, right turn off the A590

Admission charged

Opening times	1 April-end October, *Castle:* Monday, Wednesday, Thursday, Sunday — 2pm-5.45pm *Grounds:* Open from 12.30pm
Facilities	🚗; WC ; shop; tea room
Other places of interest	★Kendal Castle *(see p39)*, 3 miles north, via A591 and A6 ★The Museum of Lakeland Life and Industry, Kendal *(see p36)*, and Abbot Hall *(see p33)* ★Levens Hall, about 2 miles south on A6 ★Heron Corn Mill, 5 miles south on A6 at Beetham, via Milnthorpe ★Leighton Hall, 9½ miles south on A6, turn off at Yealand Conyers

Windermere via Staveley 13m.

KENDAL

A591

SIZERGH CASTLE

A6 (T)

A591 (T)

Levens 2½m.

M6 Junction 36 5½m.

Town Hall, Highgate, Kendal, Cumbria
☎ (0539) 25758

Abbot Hall, Kendal

The 'Auld Grey Town' of Kendal with its grey limestone buildings is situated in the valley of the River Kent. This famous Cumbrian town — the gateway to south Lakeland — has an impressive history. The Romans built a fort, south of the town (possibly called Alavna). The Normans built a motte and bailey castle in the 11th century and in the 12th century a castle was built on a hill to the east of the town by the then Baron of Kendal, Gilbert Fitz-Reinfred. The Parr family lived at the castle at the time of Katherine's birth. She was later to become the sixth wife of Henry VIII. From the ruins of the castle a panoramic view of the town may be obtained. Kendal's oldest occupied house, strangely called 'Castle Dairy' can be seen in Wildman Street. It is said Flemish weavers — the 'founding fathers' of the wool trade — made Kendal their home in the 14th century; this marked the genesis of Kendal's prosperity which soon had an international reputation for its green cloth. By the mid-1700s, Kendal was one of the most prosperous towns in the north producing everything from cloth and leatherware to snuff. By 1756 a stagecoach service was in operation between Kendal and the nation's capital. Today, Kendal produces a diverse range of products from shoes to woollen garments to carpets — and of course, mintcake!

Towards the close of the 11th century Ivo Taillebois granted the Church and lands to Benedictine Monks in the area of Kendal, called Kirkland. During the Middle Ages a house was built for the Abbot of St Mary's of York and so the dwelling became known as 'Abbot Hall'.

Now Abbot Hall in Kirkland is reputed to be one of the top art galleries in the area. It is adjacent to the parish church of Holy Trinity (a huge sanctuary of five aisles and double the number of bells) and stands on the bank of the River Kent.

In 1588, a grammar school was built on some of the Hall's land and this can still be seen. The old Abbot hall was bought by Lt-Col George Wilson who promptly demolished it. Two years later, the elegant Georgian building which can be seen today was built for £8,000. Until recently, it was acknowledged that John Carr, a much admired architect of his day, was responsible for the building, but this fact is now open to dispute. The Hall was sold to a surgeon named John Taylor in 1772; he died 12 years later. Over the course of the next century, the Hall was owned by a number of families until 1897 when joint owners Harry Arnold and Christopher Fell sold the property to the Kendal Corporation. During the 1950s with famous fell walking writer Alfred Wainwright as treasurer fund raising commenced for the restoration of the Hall and its subsequent conversion to an art gallery. Late in September 1962, Princess Margaret and Lord Snowdon formally declared Abbot Hall open to the public and early in 1974 a new gallery area was made available in the south wing.

Left:
In the Gower family room can be found the square piano of banded mahogany (c1840).

Right:
Abbot Hall

Below:
**The hall with original
pillars and Gillow furniture.**

There are four galleries upstairs which house ever changing exhibitions, ranging from fine paintings to pottery, sculpture and prints. All the rooms on the ground floor have been skilfully restored to their Georgian splendour with typical decor and furniture. The Hall retains its original pillars. Amongst the furniture here is a c1820 Gillow Mahogany table and splendid long case clocks. Fine examples of Gillow furniture feature throughout: in the breakfast room (which has been furnished in painted wood panelling) there is a writing desk; in the library a low wardrobe, and in the dining room a drop-front secretaire of rich mahogany.

The library houses Turner's 'The Passage of the St Gothard' (1804) and the original dining room exhibits George Romney's masterpiece 'The Gower Family', an oil on canvas painted 1776/77. There are also watercolours by 19th century artist John Ruskin of Brantwood, Coniston and many others.

For many years, Abbot Hall's exhibitions have toured to museums and galleries throughout the British Isles. During your visit to the gallery, you will soon realise why Abbot Hall has fast earned a name for itself as one of the leading art galleries not only in the north, but in Britain as a whole.

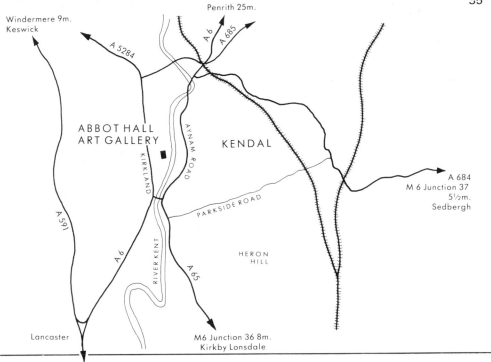

Further information

Abbot Hall   *OS Sheet 97, Ref SD 517922*

Enquiries	Abbot Hall, Kirkland, Kendal, Cumbria LA9 5AL ☎ (0539) 22464
Location	In Kirkland (at the southern end of Kendal), across the way from The Museum of Lakeland Life and Industry and next to Holy Trinity Parish Church on the bank of the River Kent
How to get there	From M6 Junction 36, A591 and then A6 into Kendal

Admission charged

Opening times	Monday-Friday 10.30am-5 pm Saturday 2pm-5pm (10.30am-5pm from Spring Bank Holiday to 31 October)

Sunday 2pm-5pm
(Closed New Year's Day, Good Friday, Christmas Day and Boxing Day)
Shop at Abbot Hall: Monday-Saturday, 10.30am-5pm

Facilities	🚗; ; refreshments in town centre
Other places of interest	★The Museum of Lakeland Life and Industry, Kendal *(see p36)*, across the way ★Kendal Castle *(see p39)*, reached via Parr Street ★The Castle Dairy in Wildman Street

Town Hall, Highgate, Kendal, Cumbria
☎ (0539) 25758 (for up-to-date information on what to see and do in Kendal and elsewhere in the Lakes)

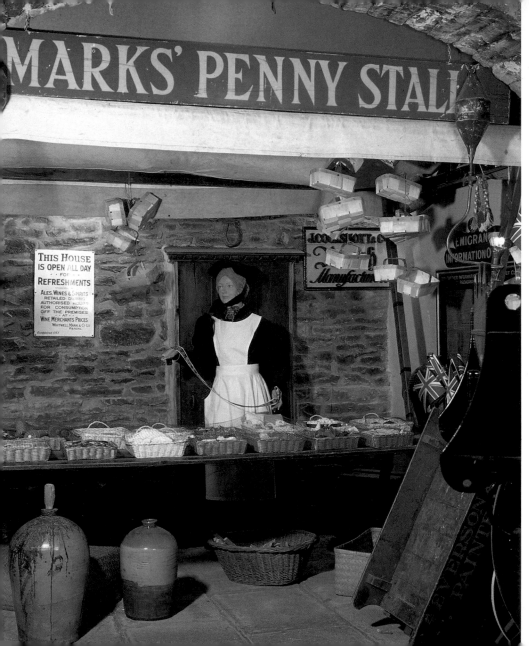

The Museum of Lakeland Life and Industry (Kendal)

Just across the way from Abbot Hall Art Gallery and housed in the 18th century stable block is The Museum of Lakeland Life and Industry, opened to the public by HRH Princess Alexandra in the Spring of 1971.

The room sets and workshops have been brilliantly reconstructed to show virtually every facet of Lakeland life from local industries, crafts and agriculture through to fashion and the domestic scene and, together with numerous photographs and comprehensive written details, tell the visitor something about the social and economic progression of bygone Lakeland to the present day.

Although many made a living from mining and quarrying, for Lakeland people the main source of income was from the wool and cloth trade. The hand loom on display is a century old and serves not only to emphasise how important these trades were in the local economy, but also to remind us that Kendal itself built up an international reputation for its quality cloth (hence, 'Kendal Green'). A local weaver is seen in a pre-World War 1 photograph working his loom and is a sad reminder of how the exponential increase in mechanisation was to take a heavy toll on many of the traditional industries. The parlour was a room reserved for use on Sundays and for special occasions — for example, a wedding. The parlour walls have been papered in late Victorian style. The pole screen in this neat little room was designed primarily to prevent women who sat too close to the fire from damaging their complexions.

Upstairs, there is a collection of kitchen utensils and a display of irons. A late 19th century handbill gives, amongst others, the price of oat bread at 4d per lb. A common use for the hanging kettle, which can be seen on the top landing, was to heat the water for baths. A black and white picture in the bedroom is of Isabella Curwen of Belle Isle, Windermere. The Brownes, yeomen farmers from Troutbeck, crafted the dressing table and also the mirror which hangs above the fireplace some time before the turn of the 19th century. The bedroom curtains are of patchwork; in one corner is an oak chest which was used to keep all the bedding in. Women would spend many an hour sewing in the bedroom. There is a small display of dresses which covers the female fashion trends from late Georgian times through to the present day. The old Grammar School houses a collection of Arthur Ransome's belongings, the author of *Swallows and Amazons*. In the south wing the visitor will find a collection of items from trades and industries of a bygone era; the reconstruction of the smithy is a marvel; one can almost hear the rhythmical clanking of the hammer as it strikes the anvil and visualise the sparks darting around the workshop. The blacksmith and wheelwright often worked in close co-operation when jobs such as wheel tyreing required the combined skills of both men.

Other displays include shoemaking, a mining display of which an exhibition of samples of finished Lake District slate forms a part — and bobbin making. The bobbin industry developed out of the Lancashire textile industry's demand for wooden bobbin reels. Bobbin mills sprang up all over the Lakes, near to the raw materials — birch and ash from the Furness coppice woods — and also near a ready supply of water to drive the waterwheels, which in turn drove the machinery. The invention of the plastic bobbin reel spelled disaster for the wooden bobbin industry and many mills closed down. However, plastic is an oil derivative. There is only a finite supply of oil and as our own North Sea stocks dwindle we are having to rely more on imported stocks from the Middle East, which of course cost a lot more. This fact coupled with an increasing interest in local trades has meant a dramatic comeback for the traditional wooden bobbin industry.

The Braithwaite bobbin-turning device stands proudly on display. It was capable of producing 20 bobbins every minute.

The array of farming equipment in the Farm Barn extension includes ploughs and a wooden harrow. One cannot emphasise too strongly how important sheep farming has been in the economy of the area, not only for lamb and mutton but also for wool. In this latter respect we are shown a clipping stool, old handclippers and a sheep dip, which is used to protect the sheep's skin from parasitic attack.

A tour of the Museum is like a blast into the past and is one full of nostalgia. It is not hard to appreciate why the Museum of Lakeland Life and Industry was judged the 'Museum of The Year' in 1973 — the first holder of the award!

Far left:
A Marks & Spencer penny bazaar of 1890.

Left:
G. M. Jennings' wheelright works.

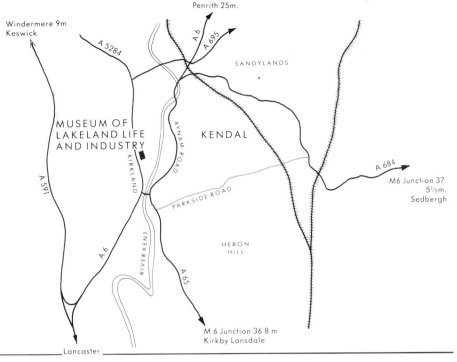

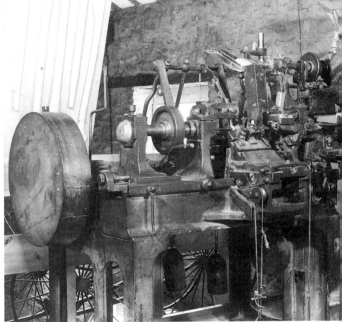

Further information

The Museum of Lakeland Life and Industry
OS Sheet 97, Ref SD 517922

Enquiries   Abbot Hall, Kirkland, Kendal, Cumbria
LA9 5AL ☎ (0539) 22464

Location   In Kirkland, Kendal, next to Holy Trinity
Parish Church and just across the way from
Abbot Hall, on the bank of the River Kent

How to get   From M6 Junction 36, A591 and then A6
there   into Kendal

Admission charged

Above right:
**At the top of the stairs, the
Braithwaite bobbin turner
(built 1881) could 'rough
out' 20 bobbins every
minute.**

Opening   Monday–Friday 10.30am–5pm
times   Saturday 2pm–5pm
(10.30am–5pm from Spring Bank Holiday to
31 October)
Sunday 2pm–5pm
(Closed — New Year's Day, Good Friday,
Christmas Day, Boxing Day)

Facilities   🚗; **WC**; refreshments in close proximity

Other   ★Abbot Hall *(see p33)*, across the way
places of   ★Kendal Castle *(see p39)*, via Parr Street
interest   ★Castle Dairy, in Wildman Street

 Town Hall, Highgate, Kendal, Cumbria
☎ (0539) 25758 (for up-to-date information on
what to see and do in Kendal and elsewhere in
the Lakes)

Kendal Castle

On the east bank of the River Kent is situated the ruins of a motte and bailey castle, perched on a hill 170ft (52m) high which commands a magnificent view of the town of Kendal, known as the 'Gateway to the South Lakes'.

The castle dates back to the late 12th century, when the Barony of Kendal passed, on the death of William de Lancaster II, to Gilbert Fitz-Reinfred (William's son-in-law). Like so many Lakeland castles and fortified dwellings, Kendal Castle was built to withstand the Scots' raids during the troubled times of border conflict.

The history of the castle and its occupancy is very patchy, even the exact date of building is not clear. What is known is that Gilbert was among those who in 1215 helped to seal the Magna Carta. Three centuries later the castle was owned by Thomas Parr, whose daughter Katherine, born within the walls in 1513, was later to become the sixth wife of Henry VIII and the only spouse to survive the great Tudor monarch.

The visible remains consist of the perimeter or curtain wall, parts of four towers, the northeast wall of the banqueting hall, one or two cellars and a large dry moat, now completely grassed over. In the northwest corner is a circular guard tower with an east-facing entrance, opening into the castle grounds. The walls of this tower are almost 6ft thick. The remains of a much smaller drum tower may be found to the southwest, and to the south the remains of a keep. To the northeast the ruins of the square tower are quite impressive. A small part of the great hall may be seen. Between the northeast and northwest towers would have been a gatehouse, with a drawbridge across the moat, facing north; all traces have now vanished. The Lords' apartments would have been situated between the gatehouse and the upper chambers in the northeast corner. Firing slits or loopholes are located in all four towers supporting the theory that this castle's main purpose was for defence.

Whilst in this historic town — which used to be the largest in old Westmorland and is famous for its mint cake and green cloth — a stroll up to the castle ruins via Parr Street for a panoramic view of Kendal with its grey limestone buildings is to be recommended.

Below:
Looking east towards the remains of the banqueting hall.

Right:
Vaulted cellar detail, northeast corner.

Far right:
Curtain wall, west side.

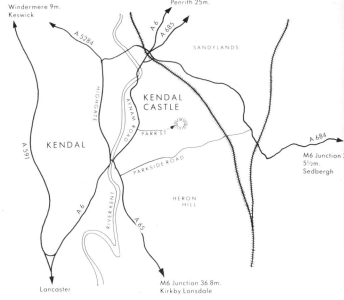

Further information

Kendal Castle   *OS Sheet 97, Ref SD 522924*

Location	On a hill to the east of the town, reached via Parr Street
How to get there	From M6 Junction 36, A591, A6 turn off into Kendal
Other places of interest	★Abbot Hall *(see p33)*, in Kirkland, Kendal ★The Museum of Lakeland Life and Industry in Kirkland, Kendal ★Castle Dairy, in Wildman Street

 Town Hall, Highgate, Kendal, Cumbria
☎ (0539) 25758 (for up-to-date information on what to see and do in Kendal and elsewhere in the Lakes)

Belle Isle, Windermere

Belle Isle, the home of Mrs E. H. S. Curwen, is situated on the island of the same name. At 38 acres, Belle Isle is the largest island on Lake Windermere, virtually dividing the lake into two. The house is circular in design, 54ft (16.5m) in diameter and is reputed to be the only one of its kind in the country.

A settlement has existed on the island since Roman times. The Norsemen called it 'Long Holm' and indeed the first family here, the Philipsons (Royalist sympathisers in the Civil War) also adopted the name. Three families, the Braithwaites, the Floyers and the Barlows owned the island after the Philipsons, until 1774 when a Mr English bought the island. With the help of an architect named John Plaw, he set about building the round Georgian mansion, with its domed roof, using local Ecclerigg Stone. It is this fine building which can be seen today. Plaw designed the house around Rome's Villa Rotunda at Vicenza (by Palladio). Plans of John Plaw's round house appeared in a publication entitled *Rural Architecture* in 1794. In designing such a home, Plaw set out to make it the focal point in the surrounding landscape. Unfortunately the building which took six years to complete was subjected to fierce criticism by conservationists who saw the new dwelling as a blot on the landscape. The great Lakeland bard William Wordsworth once described the house as 'a pepper pot'. In 1781 English sold the house to the Workington Hall heiress — 16 year-old Isabella Curwen — for £1,720, incurring a loss of more than £4,000! This young and — judging by George Romney's portrait of her — very attractive girl, eloped to Edinburgh in 1782 to marry her cousin, John Christian, who was 10 years her senior (after the couple had failed in their attempt to persuade the Lord Chancellor to grant them permission to marry). John Christian was the cousin of the famous ringleader of the *Bounty* mutineers, Fletcher Christian (who was born in Cockermouth). John Christian assumed the Curwen name by Royal Licence and on their return to Belle Isle, Mr and Mrs John Christian Curwen set about

Far left:
The dining room.

Left:
Belle Isle.

Right:
The drawing room, displaying Romney's portrait of the young Isabella Curwen.

Far right:
The Belle Isle.

the planting of woodlands, so the house would become more discreet in its surrounding environment.

The frontispiece is very impressive, with an elaborate portico which incorporates a flight of steps to the entrance. The portico ceiling bears the Curwen arms. On each side of the portico are niches which house the elegant 'summer' and 'autumn' statues.

John Christian Curwen commissioned the famous Lancaster firm of Gillow to make all the furniture. The fine satinwood commode in the drawing room, worked by Gillow craftsmen, was made in 1790 for 10 guineas. Above the drawing room fireplace is a large portrait by George Romney of the beautiful 17 year-old Isabella Curwen. There is also a writing chair which once belonged to William Wordsworth.

On display next to the window in the dining room are the remains of an ancient Viking sword, unearthed when the house was under construction in 1774. Accounts relating to the building of the house also note the discovery of some old Roman armour, supporting the theory that the Romans once inhabited the island.

The house was used during World War 2 by the Admiralty for training seamen. John and Isabella Curwen's granddaughter — also called Isabella — married John Wordsworth, son of the great poet, in 1830. Their daughter Dora paid many a visit to Belle Isle. The late Mr Edward Curwen was the great-great-great-great grandson of John and Isabella.

From the east side of the island one can look across to Bowness-on-Windermere and to Ambleside. On a clear day one can look north to the 2,864ft (873m) peak of Fairfield. A tour of this wonderful circular house and island with its wooded walks (once used by the Lord of Windermere Manor back in the mid-13th century) is the highlight of many a visit to Windermere.

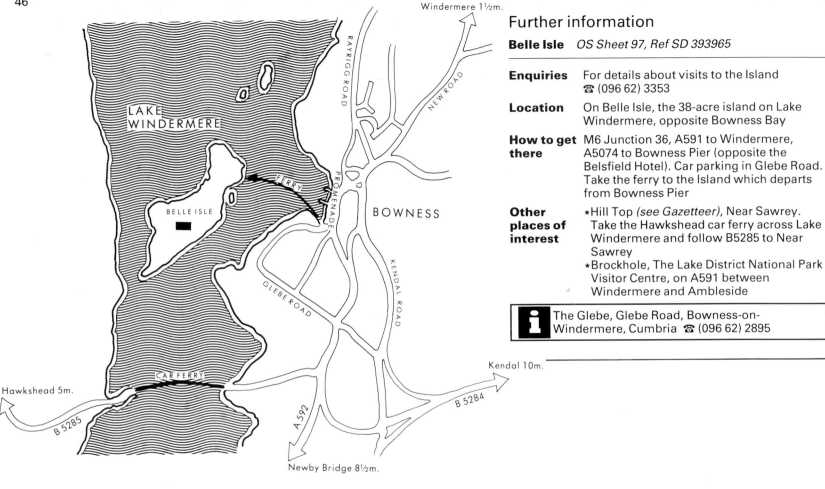

Windermere 1½m.

RAYRIGG ROAD

NEW ROAD

LAKE WINDERMERE

FERRY

PROMENADE

BELLE ISLE

BOWNESS

GLEBE ROAD

KENDAL ROAD

CAR FERRY

Hawkshead 5m.

B 5285

A 592

Newby Bridge 8½m.

B 5284

Kendal 10m.

Further information

Belle Isle   *OS Sheet 97, Ref SD 393965*

Enquiries
For details about visits to the Island
☎ (096 62) 3353

Location
On Belle Isle, the 38-acre island on Lake Windermere, opposite Bowness Bay

How to get there
M6 Junction 36, A591 to Windermere, A5074 to Bowness Pier (opposite the Belsfield Hotel). Car parking in Glebe Road. Take the ferry to the Island which departs from Bowness Pier

Other places of interest
★Hill Top *(see Gazetteer)*, Near Sawrey. Take the Hawkshead car ferry across Lake Windermere and follow B5285 to Near Sawrey
★Brockhole, The Lake District National Park Visitor Centre, on A591 between Windermere and Ambleside

i The Glebe, Glebe Road, Bowness-on-Windermere, Cumbria ☎ (096 62) 2895

Southwest Lakeland

Previous page:
Stott Park Bobbin Mill.

Right:
Silver birch poles in the coppice barns.

Far right:
Albert Graham demonstrates 'pall pealing' — the stripping of bark from the coppice poles.

Stott Park Bobbin Mill

The bobbin mill at Stott Park is located at the southern end of Lake Windermere (on the road from Lakeside to Esthwaite Water and Hawkshead) about half a mile north of Finsthwaite and very close to Newby Bridge.

It was built in 1835 by John Harrison, a farmer with strong Furness roots and was worked right up until its closure in 1971. The birth of bobbin mills was a direct response to the huge demand created by the textile industry, mostly in Lancashire, for bobbins of all shapes and sizes needed for holding thread, twine and wire. Prior to mid-19th century innovations in bobbin machinery by Messrs Braithwaite and Fell — which enabled bobbins to be sculptured from one block of wood — bobbins used to be assembled with glue in several stages. Mills also diversified to produce, amongst other things, tool handles and pulleys. During the 1950s Stott Park Mill was mass-producing the so-called spout bobbin, a circular bobbin block which was sandwiched between a drainpipe and wall (to which the former was affixed). It was economical to site the mills near to the source of raw materials (birch and ash) and also near to an abundant supply of fast-flowing water needed to drive the machinery which carved out the bobbins. At Stott Park a waterwheel formerly generated the power for the individual machines, which are connected to the drive-shaft by means of belts and pulleys. A turbine superseded the waterwheel in 1858. Towards the latter stages of the 19th century another turbine was introduced. In 1931, a third turbine was in operation, working alongside the steam engine. A brace of electric motors installed during World War 2 replaced the now defunct, late-19th century steam engine. The turbine was kept as a back-up.

After John Harrison built the mill at Stott Park, he and his brother Myles leased it out. The mill together with the Harrison lands around Low Stott Park Farm passed from the widow of Myles Harrison to the grandson, Thomas Newby Wilson. When he died in 1915, Stott Park Mill was purchased by the long-standing tenants, the Cowards. In 1855 the leaseholder of Stott Park Mill was one Thomas Eyes, a native of Kirkby Lonsdale who married Susannah

Coward. During the 1860s Thomas and Susannah bought a bobbin mill at Crooklands, south of Kendal; this move enabled Susannah's sister Elizabeth, and Elizabeth's son William Coward, to take charge of Stott Park. Mother and son subsequently undertook an extensive programme of alterations at the mill, which was once again leased out. Generations of fathers and sons laboured side by side in the mill — a dusty and often harmful working environment. Lung complaints were rife. The hours were long and fatiguing and the remuneration was but a mere pittance; for boys, schoolwork often took its toll — but for many, with little or no prospect of seeking alternative employment, this was a necessary existence.

The Cowards were powerful people in the local community, owning many properties in the surrounding Finsthwaite area. After William Coward's death in 1882 brother John took over the lease. When he died in 1917 the lease was taken over by John, William Coward's son. Four years later, John Coward purchased Stott Park Mill for £4,000. Sole progeny, the late John Robert Moncrieff Coward took over the business when his father died in 1954 and kept it going until it closed in 1971.

After felling, the birch and ash would be carted to the mill from the coppice woods and stored, either in coppice barns or outside in the yard. The so-called coppice poles would then be cut into various lengths as required. The wood was divided into 'stacks' according to the size of bobbin needed; a machine would then bore a hole through the centre of each end. Next, the roughing lathe cut the wood to approximate length, shape and diameter — the raw material was usually cut when it was wet and finished when it was dry. Once dried, bobbins were turned on finishing lathes and an array of cutting tools would then mould the bobbin exactly to meet each customer's needs. During the final process the bobbins would be placed into a polishing barrel along with some paraffin wax and turned. After half an hour, the bobbins would emerge 'varnished'.

The closure of the Mill at Stott Park marked the end of an era, for not only was it one of the last to cease operation in the Lakes, but its closure finally severed the once strong connection between the local inhabitants who worked in the mills, and the mill owners.

Right:
Polishing barrel, first floor.

Far right:
The mill floor, with machinery and leather belting.

Today, Stott Park is a working museum and the visitor can follow the bobbins through their various stages of manufacture and appreciate something of the noise and atmosphere of a Lakeland bobbin mill in its heyday. The machinery is skilfully operated by the mill's technicians, Jim Dixon and David Steeley, both of whom have well in excess of 30 years experience working in the bobbin industry and who are a mine of practical information.

Further information

Stott Park Bobbin Mill   *OS Sheet 97, Ref SD 373883*
English Heritage Site   (0448) 31087

Further enquiries	Abbot Hall, Kirkland, Kendal, Cumbria LA9 5AL ☎ (0539) 22464 (managers for English Heritage)
Location	½ mile north of Finsthwaite at the southern end of Lake Windermere, on the road from Lakeside to Esthwaite Water and Hawkshead, and very close to Newby Bridge
How to get there	From M6 Junction 36, A591, A590 via Levens to Newby Bridge. The Mill is signposted — turn off A590 at Newby Bridge

Admission charged

Opening times	Good Friday-31 October Daily 10am-6pm
Facilities	🚗; **WC** ; refreshments — Lakeside and Newby Bridge
Other places of interest	★Cartmel Priory *(see p52)*, 9 miles south ★Holker Hall *(see p56)*, just over 9 miles south, via A590 to Haverthwaite and then B5278

 Hawkshead ☎ (09666) 525
The Glebe, Glebe Road, Bowness-on-Windermere ☎ (096 62) 2895 (during season)

Windermere 10m

STOTT PARK BOBBIN MILL

WINDERMERE

A 592

LAKESIDE

RIVER LEVEN

NEWBY BRIDGE

A 590

A 590

Ulverston 9½m.

M6 Junction 36 via Levens 18m.

Cartmel Priory Church

The huge Priory church with its diagonal towers stands in the little village of Cartmel on the peninsula of the same name, protruding out into Morecambe Bay on the borders of South Lakeland. The church of St Mary and St Michael, with a seating capacity of around 450, almost dwarfs the surrounding village. Worshippers have been coming here for 800 years ever since the Earl of Pembroke, William Marshall — intrepid knight and top adviser to King John at the signing of the Magna Carta — founded the large sanctuary for the Augustinian (Black) Canons in 1188. The first canons to inhabit the priory originated from the Wiltshire village of Bradenstoke near Chippenham. With the church came the lands of Cartmel which stretched as far as Windermere and passed into the ownership of George Preston of Holker Hall. They have been passed down by descent and today they are in the hands of the Cavendish family. After lands had been granted, building of the north and south transepts and the choir commenced.

At the Dissolution of the Monasteries in 1536, many church buildings were destroyed. Surprisingly, the Norman Priory and gatehouse were not too badly scarred. The church roof was dismantled, but the Town Choir was untouched, probably because William Marshall had stipulated, when providing lands, that the inhabitants of Cartmel must have a sanctuary in which to worship God.

The church lay partially in ruins until 1620 when George Preston undertook restoration work, a period which saw the rebuilding of the church roof. (The Preston memorial may be seen in the nave.) He brought in the

Far left:
Cartmel Priory

Below left:
One of many carved misericords (c1440) to be found in the choir. This particular one depicts a double-tailed mermaid.

Below:
The Cavendish memorial.

Right:
Stained glass in the huge east window dates from c1420.

Far right:
A view of Cartmel village from the tower looking east towards Hampsfield Fell.

huge oak screen for the choir. Beneath this screen are the lovely misericords, dating from c1440, which offered support to tired monks. Each misericord bears a different carving. One bears a double-tailed mermaid, another shows a griffin and an elephant and castle. The church interior has many other features of interest: the massive east window has dimensions of 45ft (13.7m) by 23ft (7m). Some of the glass is contemporary with the misericords (c1440); there are the remains of the Harrington Tomb. The nave was constructed in the early part of the 15th century; next to the choir and on its north side is the Piper Choir, an ancient survival. The chevrons incorporated into the pointed entrance arch indicate the work of Norman craftsmen; part of the Piper Choir's roof is original stone. The brass chandelier dates from 1734. In the Town Choir of the church is the early 13th century font, which was remodelled in the Victorian period. The cover dates from 1640. In the north corner is the memorial to the 7th Duke of Devonshire's son, Lord Frederick Cavendish — a high-ranker in the Cabinet of W. E. Gladstone; he was in charge of Irish affairs. Lord Frederick was murdered in Dublin's Phoenix Park in 1882.

The two diagonal towers, seemingly an architectural hiccup, attract a lot of attention. The tremendous load exerted by these twin features is skilfully directed to the Banstable Slate foundation through a carefully designed composition of arches and columns. The tower contains a new peal of six bells installed in 1988, together with two ancient bells.

Because the Priory has undergone quite a few restoration programmes throughout the ages, it is important to realise that its interior is a reflection of different styles of architecture.

The Rev William Taylor, the poet William Wordsworth's old headmaster at Hawkshead Grammar School, is buried in the graveyard. The original entrance to Cartmel Priory was the gatehouse (built c1340 and now owned by the National Trust) which the visitor can see in Cavendish Street. Following restoration at the Priory, the local school acquired this lucky survival of the Dissolution from Holker's George Preston.

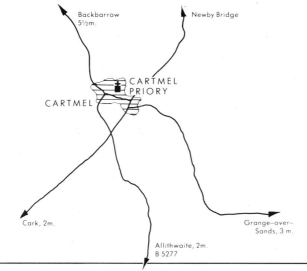

Backbarrow 5½ m.

Newby Bridge

CARTMEL PRIORY

CARTMEL

Cark, 2 m.

Grange-over-Sands, 3 m.

Allithwaite, 2 m.
B 5277

Further information

Cartmel Priory   *OS Sheet 97, Ref SD 380788*

Location	In the centre of Cartmel Village on the Cartmel Peninsula (Priory Gatehouse is in Cavendish Street — National Trust Site)
How to get there	From M6 Junction 36, A591, A6, A590 via Levens. Turn off A590 on to B5277 to Grange-over-Sands. Follow signs to Cartmel
Opening times	Summer: 8.30am-5.30pm Winter: 8.30am-3.30pm
Facilities	🚗; **WC**; refreshments in the village
Other places of interest	★Holker Hall *(see p56)*, just over 2 miles southwest ★Stott Park Bobbin Mill *(see p48)*, 9 miles to the north, via Newby Bridge

i Victoria Hall, Main Street, Grange-over-Sands, Cumbria ☎ (044 84) 4026 (during season)

Holker Hall

Holker Hall, home of the Prestons, Lowthers and residence of the Cavendishs (a family with Suffolk roots) for more than 200 years, can be found west of Grange-over-Sands at Cark-in-Cartmel. The history can be traced back to before the Dissolution when the lands were once owned by the influential Cartmel Priory. In about 1556 the Preston family stepped in and acquired the Holker lands. George Preston — who restored much of the huge Priory Church at Cartmel, bringing in the fine renaissance screens — laid the foundations in 1604 for the building of a hall. In 1644 George Preston's son and heir, Thomas, was forced to pay excessive fines as a punishment for playing host to Royalist soldiers at the Hall. The legacy then passed to Catherine, Thomas's daughter in 1697. In that same year, Catherine married Sir William Lowther whose heir, Sir Thomas Lowther, was later to marry one of the 2nd Duke of Devonshire's daughters, Lady Elizabeth Cavendish (Lady Elizabeth's great-great-great grandfather, Sir William Cavendish was married to 'Bess of Hardwick'). (Elizabeth Hardwick — a woman of substance — injected power and wealth into the Cavendish family, bringing in estates bequeathed to her by her father and by her first husband in the mid-16th century.) Sir Thomas Lowther was responsible for the rebuilding programmes at Holker which were undertaken in around 1720 which included the layout of the gardens and the construction of a north wing. Sir Thomas's son, Sir William, was a good friend of the artist Sir Joshua Reynolds and brought in many paintings to the Hall. As a result of Sir William's celibacy, Holker Hall passed in 1756 to Lord George Augustus Cavendish, his first cousin (Lord George Augustus' father was the 3rd Duke of Devonshire; his aunt, Lady Elizabeth Cavendish was Sir William Lowther's mother.) It can be seen that since the mid-16th century when the Prestons first lived at the Hall, through to the Lowthers and Cavendish's occupancy, the house has never passed hands by sale: it has always been inherited (all three families are related) through the generations, and so to the current owners, Mr and Mrs Hugh Cavendish.

Lord George Augustus, a long serving MP, commissioned York architect John Carr to build a Gothic-style east wing between 1783 and 1793. Many alterations were made to the grounds at this time. Lord George Augustus' son, Lord George Augustus Henry Cavendish, later to be made the Earl of Burlington in 1831, inherited the estates in 1803 and undertook yet more alterations giving the frontispiece a Roman cement facing. When the Earl of Burlington died in 1835 the legacy passed to William Cavendish, his grandson; William, at the time of his inheritance, was the 2nd Earl of Burlington. He was later to become the 7th Duke of Devonshire. The alterations which the 7th Duke undertook included the building of a conservatory and stable and the refacing of the whole house.

Tenth March 1871 was a disastrous day at Holker: whilst the family were locked in slumber, a fire broke out in the west wing. By the time the 7th Duke and his family had been roused, the fire had become an uncontrollable inferno and by first light it was clear that the west wing had been completely incinerated. Priceless treasures, which included much of Sir Thomas Lowther's early 18th century collection of paintings and items of furniture, had all been consumed by the fire. All had been lost, except a carpet which was thrown out of the window (now in Queen Mary's Dressing Room — you can still see the scorch marks!) and a marble pedestal — which looked to be intact, but which shattered as soon as the 7th Duke's son tried to move it. Pieces of the marble were later used in the Hall's chimney piece.

The 7th Duke set the wheels in motion for the rebuilding of a new and magnificent west wing to begin immediately and the Lancaster-based firm of Paley & Austin, architects of national repute, were commissioned for the job. The new wing was constructed on the same site as the old west wing, with one or two additions which include Holker's landmark, the Copper Cupola. The wing took four years to construct and the date of completion, 1875, may be seen on one of the panels to the left of the hall fireplace. This new Victorian wing, finished in red sandstone, stands as a paragon and is a tribute to the architects and craftsmen who worked at length with true dedication.

The drawing room walls are hung with silk, which dates from 1875. The room contains a variety of different furniture, which includes Chippendale and Hepplewhite. An interesting painting entitled 'Storm at Sea', was originally one of a brace which Sir William Lowther commissioned in Rome. The other, entitled 'Calm Sea', was lost in the fire. The library with its fine linenfold panelling houses in excess of 3,500 books. There are accounts by Henry Cavendish, a grandson of the 2nd Duke of Devonshire. Henry Cavendish spent his whole life sequestered away, dedicated to science; amongst other things, he discovered nitric acid. There are many portraits of the Cavendish Family in this room; the dining room, too, houses a large number of family portraits. Of special note is the fireplace with its twisted columns crafted in local oak. The large oak cantilever staircase is undoubtedly the highlight of the interior in the opinion of the author. This self-supporting structure, elegant in its

Far left:
The oak cantilever staircase.

Below left:
Queen Mary's room.

Below:
Holker Gardens, with the monkey puzzle tree in the top left of the picture.

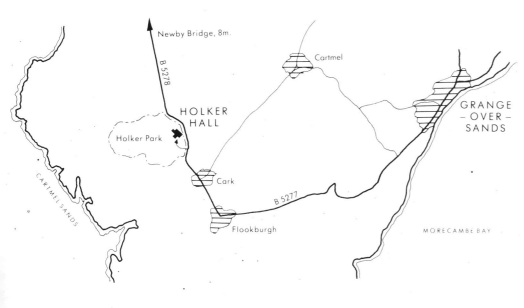

Victorian design, was worked by craftsmen from nearby. The Hall is home to portraits of Charles I and James II. The Duke's Bedroom was used by William Cavendish, the 7th Duke of Devonshire in the latter stages of his life; he died in 1891 at the age of 83. His wife died when he was only 32 and he never married again. His distinctions included being made a Knight of the Garter and a Chancellor of Cambridge University. A picture of the one-time 2nd Earl of Burlington, clothed in his Chancellor's gown, can be found next to the bed. During his occupancy at Holker Hall, the 7th Duke bred the Shorthorn Cow; he marketed 30 head of cattle in 1878 for nearly £20,000 — a princely sum even today! The window looks out over the garden and gives a superb view of the Parkland beyond. In the gallery, they used to play carpet bowls.

Holker Hall is surrounded by 22 acres of gardens. There is also a deer park of 120 acres. The unique Monkey Puzzle tree was uprooted at the end of the 19th century and had to be re-rooted and anchored in stones and cement. As well as the interior and spacious grounds, Holker has exhibitions of old Lake District trades and a display of kitchen ware from the Victorian, Edwardian and World War 2 eras. There is also The Lakeland Motor Museum having a wonderful collection of vintage motor cars.

Further information

Holker Hall   *OS Sheet 97, Ref SD 359774*
House and 22 acres of gardens; 120-acre deer park; Craft and Countryside Museum; playground; baby animal house; Lakeland Motor Museum; hot air balloons

Enquiries	Holker Hall, Cark-in-Cartmel, Grange-over-Sands, Cumbria LA11 7PL ☎ (044 853) 328
Location	West of Grange-over-Sands, about 2 miles southwest of Cartmel
How to get there	From M6 Junction 36, A591, A590 to Haverthwaite via Newby Bridge. At Haverthwaite, take B5278 following signs to Holker

Admission charged

Opening times	10.30am-6pm. Easter Day — Last Sunday in October Last admission to grounds and Hall 4.30pm
Facilities	🚗; WC; café; gift shop
Other places of interest	★Cartmel Priory — 2 miles to the north east ★Stott Park Bobbin Mill — 9 miles north via B5278 to Haverthwaite, then A590 to Newby Bridge and thence to the Mill via the Lakeside-Hawkshead Road

 Victoria Hall, Main Street, Grange-over-Sands, Cumbria ☎ (044 84) 4026 (during season)

Swarthmoor Hall

The Elizabethan Hall, famous for its close ties with the Quaker movement, is located about one mile south of Ulverston. It was built in 1586 by George Fell, a wealthy landowner, whose estates were once owned by Furness Abbey.

George's son, Judge Thomas Fell, brought his wife Margaret to the Hall in 1632. George Fox, founder of The Religious Society of Friends (better known as The Quakers), first came to Swarthmoor in 1652 during a preaching tour. The Hall always had an open door to visiting preachers, but the church during this period was going through a difficult time. Independents and Presbyterians were constantly trying to get the better of one another. Simultaneously, sectarian groups started to spring up all over the place and were subsequently frowned upon by church ministers, who thought that their parishioners would be distracted from following the 'right path'. This was also the age when accusations of witchcraft (for which a person could be sentenced to death) were rife, and so the intolerant minister of Ulverston Parish was quick to try to suppress Fox's teaching.

Nevertheless, Margaret Fell and her seven daughters were very much inspired by Fox's delivery. The Judge allowed Swarthmoor to be used as a Quaker meeting house which was run by his wife and daughters. Whilst this leviathan Judge was alive no one dared to question him, but after his passing in 1658, family and Friends alike became the target of considerable harassment. Thousands of Friends were incarcerated, and Margaret herself was later to be imprisoned in Lancaster Castle.

Margaret Fell championed the Friend's cause with a perpetual devotion, which was to culminate in her second marriage, to the great founder, George Fox, in 1669. When this man who 'Stood for God' was laid to rest in 1691, more than 2,000 Friends attended his funeral. Margaret's final years were spent at Swarthmoor under the care of her youngest daughter, Rachel, and Rachel's husband, Daniel Abraham. Margaret died in 1702, leaving the Hall in the care of Rachel and Daniel. Family

ownership of the Hall lasted until 1759 after which time the place was left to decay; the ensuing period of neglect was to last for well over 150 years until 1912, when Emma Clark Abraham, a direct descendant of Rachel and Daniel Abraham, set the wheels of the restoration process in motion. In 1954 Swarthmoor was purchased by The Religious Society of Friends.

The Hall is noted for its ornately carved oak panelling and a newel staircase which is almost unique in design, and fine carved fireplaces. During the English Civil War

Left:
The newel staircase.

Below:
George Fox's sea chest in the attic.

Roundhead soldiers are said to have slept in the attic, a room which today houses the wooden chest owned by George Fox. The garden is undoubtedly the best place to view the Hall; from here the visitor will notice the mullioned windows with diamond-shaped panes, and also the balcony which George Fox once used as a preaching platform.

At Swarthmoor the visitor will be able to appreciate the feeling of serenity — of 'sweet peace' — which is so much a part of the Quaker experience.

Far left:
Swarthmoor Hall.

Left:
Margaret Fell's bedroom.

Further information

Swarthmoor Hall *OS Sheet 96, Ref SD 282773*

Enquiries	Swarthmoor Hall, Swarthmoor, Ulverston, Cumbria LA12 0JQ ☎ (0229) 53204
Location	1 mile south of Ulverston
How to get there	From M6 Junction 36, A591, A590 via Newby Bridge and Greenodd to Ulverston. Swarthmoor Hall is well signposted at Ulverston
Admission charges	Payments towards the upkeep of the Hall and gardens are requested
Opening times	Mid-March to mid-October. Monday, Tuesday, Wednesday and Saturday 10am-noon, 2pm-5pm; Thursday and Sunday by appointment only; (Friday, closed all day)
Facilities	🚗 in the grounds; refreshments at Ulverston
Other places of interest	★Furness Abbey *(see p64)*, 6 miles southwest. A590 via Dalton-in-Furness

ℹ️ Coronation Hall, County Square, Ulverston
☎ (0229) 57120 (during season)

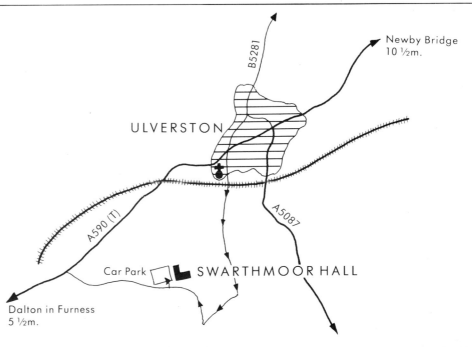

Below:
Furness Abbey.

Right:
The church and north transept.

Furness Abbey

Just over one mile north of Barrow, off the A590, are the picturesque red sandstone ruins of Furness Abbey, founded by Stephen (later to become King of England) in 1123. Some four years later the foundations were laid by the Savigny Monks who, in 1147, joined with the Cistercian order. Before moving to Furness, the Savigny brethren were originally at Tulketh, Preston.

The original entrance to this grandiose sanctuary was via the gatehouse, which lay due north of the church. Today's vast remains are certainly impressive: the transepts and choir walls to the east of the church peak almost to their original height. Most of the church dates from the mid-12th century, with various rebuilding programmes such as the eastern end of the church taking place in the late 15th century. Column bases and a portion of the original north wall are all that remain of a once colossal, late 12th century 10-bay nave. The north and south transepts date from the same period, but their windows were constructed in the 15th century; the eastern aisles of both transepts were also restructured in the 15th century. The north transept houses the base of an old tomb, and in one corner a spiral staircase may be seen. Both transepts were designed with rounded, eastern walls, each containing a small chapel. These rounded ends were later restructured and squared off.

In the Presbytery (mid/late-15th century construction), located at the easternmost end of the church, are a well-preserved and elaborate *piscina* and *sedilia* (a small basin which was used to clean the sacred vessels, and four seats for the clergy, respectively). The gigantic Presbytery east window stands in excess of 492ft (150m) high. At the opposite end to the Presbytery is the west belfry tower. Standing just short of its original height, this structure was erected around the turn of the 16th century. To the south of the church are the remains of the cloister (an area where the resident brethren would spend much of their time) originally an enclosed rectangular building. To the east of the cloister and south of the church are five beautiful arches with rounded heads. The second arch (counting along from the church)

66

gives access to the Chapter House which, until the close of the 18th century, still had its vault intact. Here column bases, like well-placed stumps, are left standing. The two arches either side of the second arch lead to vaulted chambers. The remains of the Parlour (where brethren were permitted conversation) are located due south of the Chapter House. The remains of the dorter undercroft (sleeping quarters), originally a 12-bay construction some 187ft (57m) in length and reputed to be the largest in England, may be seen south of the parlour. To the far south are the foundations of an infirmary and chapel which date from the 14th century.

The sheer size of Furness alone is indicative of the Abbey's former importance. Indeed, this Cistercian house was once the second wealthiest and most powerful in the land, surpassed only by Fountains Abbey. This opulence was derived mainly from local iron deposits, agriculture and sheep farming in and around the vicinity of the Furness Peninsula; these factors not only financed the building of the Abbey, but also enabled Furness to establish daughter houses — first at Calder (c1135) — and later further afield in Ireland.

Peace and prosperity were rudely disrupted in the early 14th century when border conflict became rife. The frequent pillaging and plundering by Scots marauders is well documented in the Lanercost Chronicle of 1316. In 1322 the resident abbot paid ransom to Robert the Bruce for the Furness District in an effort to stop this belligerence. Monies paid from the Furness coffers were a sufficient tempter to prevent the usurpation of the Abbey.

The monks of Furness relinquished their fine sanctuary to Henry VIII's men on 9 April 1537, each monk in turn placing his signature upon the document of surrender. The Chapter House marked the venue for this act of suppression. After the Dissolution, the Abbey passed to Thomas Cromwell and thence to the Curwen family, to the Prestons, the Lowthers and the Cavendishs of Holker Hall. Today the Abbey is under the protection of English Heritage, The Royal Commission on the Historic Monuments of England.

The Cistercian rule stipulated that their houses be built in isolated, uninhabited spots, and so the location of Furness on this peninsula — with the Irish sea to the south and west, Morecambe Bay to the east and the mountainous terrain of the Lake District to the north — offered the ideal place in which the monks could sequester themselves.

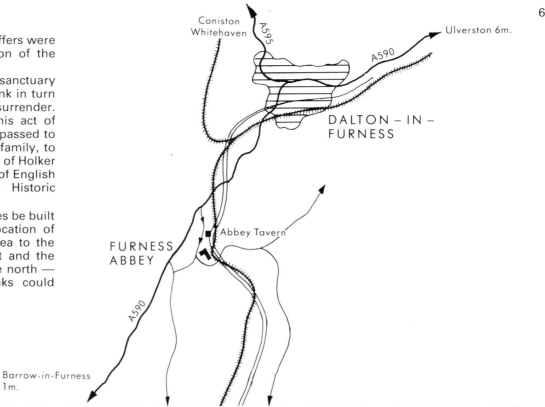

Further information

Furness Abbey   *OS Sheet 96, Ref SD 218717*
English Heritage Site

Enquiries   ☎ (0229) 23420

Location   Just over 1 mile north of Barrow-in-Furness, off the A590

How to get there   From M6 Junction 36, A591, A590 via Newby Bridge, Ulverston and Dalton-in-Furness

Admission charged

Opening times   Summer: 15 March-15 October; Monday-Saturday 9.30am-6.30pm; Sunday 2pm-6.30pm
Winter: 16 October-14 March; Monday-Saturday 9.30am-4pm; Sunday 2pm-4pm

Facilities   🚗; **WC** ; refreshments available at The Abbey Tavern (next door)

Other places of interest   *Swarthmoor Hall (see p61),* 6 miles northeast of the Abbey, near Ulverston

 Civic Hall, 28 Duke Street, Barrow-in-Furness
☎ (0229) 25795

Muncaster Castle

About one mile southeast of the Roman coastal settlement of Glannoventa (now Ravenglass) stands Muncaster Castle, a magnificent structure of pinkish granite which commands a fine view up Eskdale and across to the Scafell range. The castle has been the family home of the Penningtons for centuries. Its history goes back to the opening of the 13th century when, in 1208, Alan de Penitone was granted the lands. In around 1258 Gamel de Mulcastre laid the foundations for the building of a castle on this site. The belligerence of the Scots during the traumatic years of the border wars resulted in the construction of a defensive pele tower in 1325 (the oldest part of the present castle). In the early years of the 15th century a hall was added.

After the Battle of Hexham in 1464, Henry VI was sheltered at Muncaster by Sir John Pennington. Legend has it that, as a gesture of thanks, the king left behind a glass bowl with the proviso that so long as this bowl remained intact, the Pennington family would prosper. The famous bowl with gilt decoration is known as 'The Luck of Muncaster'.

John Pennington, First Lord Muncaster, undertook an extensive programme of restoration in 1783 which incorporated the building of a tower (referred to as 'Chapels') and the initial stages of construction of the library. This octagonal room, built on the foundations of the ancient kitchens, was improved in 1862 by an architect named Anthony Salvin as part of further renovations commissioned by John Pennington's great nephew, the Fourth Lord Muncaster, Gamel Augustus. The library's gallery houses mainly Pennington family portraits. A collection of tiny, toy-like chairs perched on top of the Elizabethan table are a quaint feature and date from the mid/late 17th century.

The much admired drawing room — also attributed to Salvin's hand — with its beautiful barrel ceiling, was redecorated in 1958. Resting on a huge Italian table the sculptured alabaster lady, is by John of Bologna and dates from around the mid-16th century. There are paintings by Sir Joshua Reynolds and Sir Thomas

Right:
John of Bologna's alabaster lady, sculpted c1550.

Far right:
Muncaster Castle.

Lawrence. The dining room, with its leather-covered walls, has a mid-17th century table, around which are a dozen Charles II chairs of walnut. A most outstanding feature of the west bedroom is the grand four-poster bed; this fine Elizabethan carved piece has ornately decorated panels. The tapestries in this room are Flemish (late 17th century). On the stairs are Canova's Three Marbles called 'The Dancing Hours', they date from about 1810.

When Josslyn Francis (Gamel Augustus' brother), 5th and last Lord Muncaster died in 1917, the estate passed to Sir John Ramsden, the nearest relative. We owe the famous rhododendrons to Sir John, which he planted after World War 1. Sir John's son, Sir William Pennington-Ramsden, gave Muncaster to his daughter Phyllida (Mrs Patrick Gordon-Duff-Pennington) in 1983.

A tour of Muncaster Castle with its splendid rooms, and spacious grounds filled with rhododendrons and azaleas, with a breathtaking view up Eskdale and the central peaks, all make for a memorable visit.

Far left:
Mid to late 17th century miniature chairs perched on the library's Elizabethan table.

Centre left:
Cromwellian bracket clock at the bottom of the staircase.

Above:
Canova's 'The Dancing Hours' (c1810), one of three marble reliefs on the staircase.

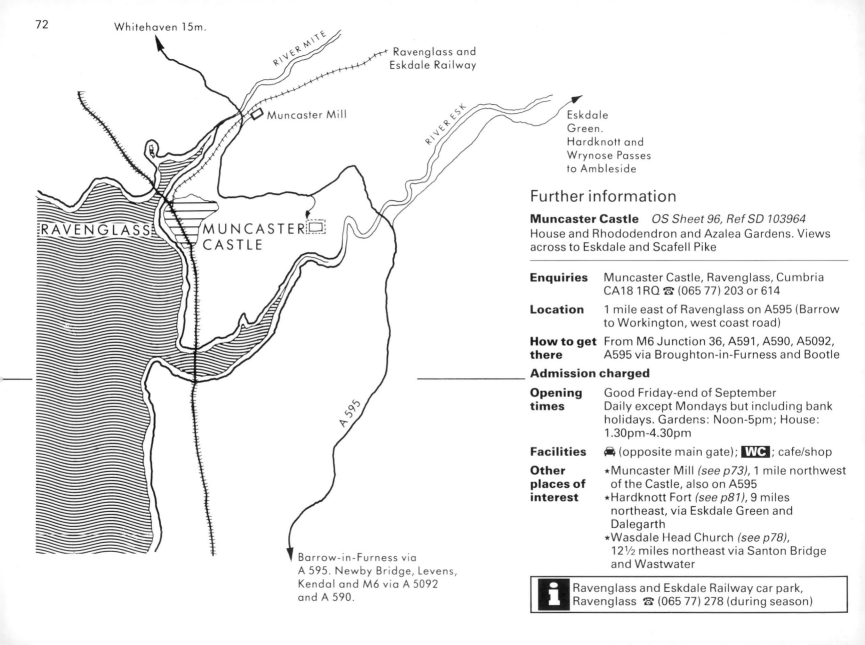

Whitehaven 15m.

RIVER MITE

Ravenglass and
Eskdale Railway

Muncaster Mill

RIVER ESK

Eskdale
Green.
Hardknott and
Wrynose Passes
to Ambleside

RAVENGLASS

MUNCASTER
CASTLE

A 595

Barrow-in-Furness via
A 595. Newby Bridge, Levens,
Kendal and M6 via A 5092
and A 590.

Further information

Muncaster Castle   *OS Sheet 96, Ref SD 103964*
House and Rhododendron and Azalea Gardens. Views
across to Eskdale and Scafell Pike

Enquiries	Muncaster Castle, Ravenglass, Cumbria CA18 1RQ ☎ (065 77) 203 or 614
Location	1 mile east of Ravenglass on A595 (Barrow to Workington, west coast road)
How to get there	From M6 Junction 36, A591, A590, A5092, A595 via Broughton-in-Furness and Bootle

Admission charged

Opening times	Good Friday-end of September Daily except Mondays but including bank holidays. Gardens: Noon-5pm; House: 1.30pm-4.30pm
Facilities	🚗 (opposite main gate); **WC**; cafe/shop
Other places of interest	★Muncaster Mill *(see p73)*, 1 mile northwest of the Castle, also on A595 ★Hardknott Fort *(see p81)*, 9 miles northeast, via Eskdale Green and Dalegarth ★Wasdale Head Church *(see p78)*, 12½ miles northeast via Santon Bridge and Wastwater

ℹ️ Ravenglass and Eskdale Railway car park,
Ravenglass ☎ (065 77) 278 (during season)

Muncaster Corn Mill

Not far from Ravenglass, the ancient Fort of Glan-noventa, on the west coast of Cumbria and situated on the banks of the Mite, is Muncaster Mill, a restored and operational corn mill dating from c1700. Although it is possible that a mill existed hereabouts in Roman times, the earliest documentary evidence at Muncaster Castle — historic seat of the Penningtons — dated 1455, notes that Thomas Senhouse leased the mill for £3 a year. In 1623 Richard Tubman, resident miller at that time, is mentioned in an 'arbitration award'. In 1735 Charles Ashley leased the present mill for £38 a year, and in 1808 John Vicers leased the property for the same sum.

Wholemeal flour for human consumption was produced here until the end of World War 1 and thereafter the mill churned out grain for cattle fodder and also oatmeal; the latter was produced until 1954.

In bygone days, long before effective transportation and communication links and steam power were ever thought of, settlements were quite isolated. The water-powered corn mill was therefore created to cater for the needs of the local community. Oats have always been much more tolerant of the upland climate and have been much easier to cultivate than barley and wheat. This climatic factor together with inefficient means of transport (to bring in these cereals) explains why these mills concentrated on the production of oatmeal in preference to the above cereals.

With the millrace and waterwheel in a dilapidated state, Muncaster Mill closed in 1961. The exponential increase in tourism, a revived interest in restored historic buildings, plus a new interest developing in stoneground products using traditional machinery, convinced the Ravenglass and Eskdale Railway Company that the purchase in 1975 and subsequent restoration of the mill under the guidance of the Eskdale [Cumbria] Trust in 1976 would be a worthwhile venture.

The waterwheel (of the 'overshot' type) of nearly 13ft in diameter has been retimbered and the millrace, about ¾-mile in length, which channels water from the River Mite, has been cleared of silt and weeds. The surfaces of

Left:
A view of the ground floor.

Far left:
Muncaster Mill.

Left:
The stone floor exhibiting three pairs of stones. From left to right: French Burr stones; millstone grit stones; shelling, or cracking stones.

Below:
Disused milling machinery on display in the yard.

the millstones have been re-cut (known as 'dressing') and most of the machinery has been restored. Milling started again in 1978 and the French stones, dating from 1845, produced wheat flour for the first time in 60 years. Today the visitor can choose from a variety of stoneground products on sale.

Because of heavy rainfall in upland areas, a kiln was needed to dry out the grain (mainly oats) prior to milling. Grain is placed on the tiled kiln floor and then hot air rises from a fire beneath through thousands of little holes in the tiles, so drying the grain. Upstairs you will find yourself in the milling area. Notice the three pairs of millstones, top part of the groat elevator and a sack hoist.

Once the oats have dried, they pass from a hopper into a pair of 'shelling' stones (on your right). These stones remove the husks from the grain and pass both down a chute to a 'wire machine', which removes the dust. Husks and grain then pass into a husking machine, containing a fan, which not only blows the husks away leaving behind the cleaned grains, but also grades the grains, known as 'groats'. High quality grains are fed upstairs by the groat elevator, leaving behind the lighter inferior grains.

The pair of 'peak stones' (ie the centre pair of three pairs of stones) are used for the fine milling of groats to oatmeal. The pair of stones to the left — known as 'Burr' stones — are for milling wheat flour.

Downstairs you can see an array of cogs and gearing which transfers the power harnessed by the waterwheel to the various pieces of machinery inside. Note also the wire machine (mentioned above) and the lower part of the groat elevator. The 'oatmeal shaker' is a device which grades the oatmeal; the 'flour dresser' grades the wholewheat flour.

In the Mill yard is a collection of milling paraphernalia. You can catch a train direct to the Mill and observe the milling process at close quarters.

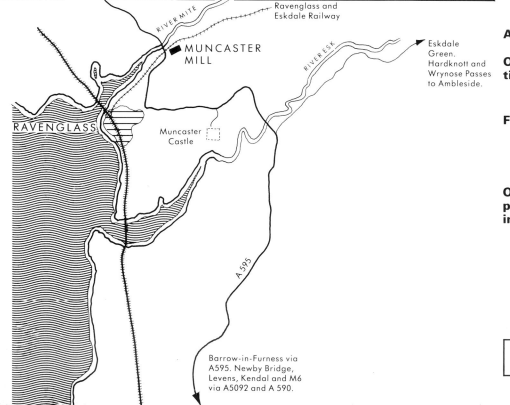

Further information

Muncaster Mill   *OS Sheet 96, Ref SD 096977*

Enquiries	The Manager, Muncaster Water Mill, Ravenglass, Cumbria CA18 1ST ☎ (065 77) 232
Location	1 mile northeast of Ravenglass (on Cumbria's west coast) and 1 mile northwest of Muncaster Castle on the A595
How to get there	From M6 Junction 36, A591, A590 via Newby Bridge, A5092, A595 (Barrow to Workington Road) via Broughton-in-Furness and Bootle

Admission charged

Opening times	Every day, except Saturdays. April, May, September 11am-5pm June, July, August 10am-6pm Other times by appointment
Facilities	; **WC** ; shop selling stoneground products; refreshments available in Ravenglass *Ravenglass and Eskdale train stops at the Mill (miniature gauge)*
Other places of interest	★Muncaster Castle *(see p68)*, 1 mile southeast on A595. ★Hardknott Fort *(see p81)*, 9 miles northeast via Eskdale Green and Dalegarth. Take first turning on right (off A595) past the mill — signposts first to Santon Bridge, then Eskdale Green. ★Wasdale Head Church *(see p78)*, 11½ miles northeast, via Santon Bridge and Wastwater

 Ravenglass and Eskdale Railway car park, Ravenglass ☎ (065 77) 278 (during season)

Northwest Lakeland

St Olaf's Church, Wasdale Head

The tiny church of St Olaf, reputed to be one of the smallest in the country, can be found in the hamlet of Wasdale Head. This small sanctuary used to serve St Bees Priory (south of Whitehaven on the west coast of Cumbria) as a chapel of ease and dates back to the 16th century. The church is situated amidst some of the most breathtaking scenery in the whole Lake District. To reach it, the visitor must take the road from Gosforth which passes through Nether Wasdale and after Wasdale Hall follows around the western shore, the whole length of Wastwater (some three miles) before entering Wasdale Head. Mountains are all around, they dominate this area of true natural beauty, an area where peak and water reconcile. At the head of Wastwater are the slopes of Yewbarrow and towering above Wasdale Head to the northeast are Kirk Fell 2,631ft (802m) and Great Gable 2,949.5ft (899m). To the east of the lake is the highest mountain in England, Scafell Pike 3,205ft (977m). The little chapel, barely 36ft (11m) long and just under 14ft (4.25m) wide, seats about 40 people. Because of its small size, the nave and chancel are one continuous feature. The church is noted for the carved oak panels and bellcote. Many climbers who have come to grief in the area are buried in the graveyard. The local inn once had a landlord called Will Ritson who was renowned for telling tall stories. This Munchausen was reported to have said that Wasdale had the deepest lake, the highest mountain, the smallest church . . . and the greatest liar in the whole county!

Right:
This etching in the south window (together with a verse from the bible . . .) is of the rock pinnacle — Napes Needle — which is located beneath Great Gable.

I WILL LIFT UP MINE EYES UNTO THE HILLS FROM WHENCE COMETH MY STRENGTH.

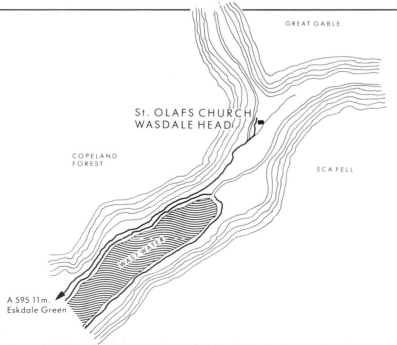

GREAT GABLE

St. OLAFS CHURCH
WASDALE HEAD

COPELAND
FOREST

SCA FELL

WAST WATER

A 595 11m.
Eskdale Green

Further information

St Olaf's Church, Wasdale Head   *OS Sheet 89, Ref NY 188087*

Location   In the hamlet of Wasdale Head, northeast of Wastwater and below the peaks of Kirk Fell and Great Gable

How to get there   From M6 Junction 36, A591 to Waterhead, then A593. Turn off A593 (signposts to Langdale and Wrynose), Wrynose and Hardknott passes, Dalegarth, Eskdale Green, Santon Bridge, Nether Wasdale and Wastwater
Note: *Wrynose and Hardknott passes unsuitable in winter/unsuitable for coaches*

Alternative route   From M6 Junction 36, A590 via Newby Bridge, A5092, A595 (Barrow to Workington road), via Broughton-in-Furness and Bootle to Muncaster Mill. Turn off the A595 beyond the Mill — signposts to Santon Bridge, then signposts to Wasdale Head

Admission free — donations appreciated

Facilities   🚗; **WC** in the hamlet; refreshments at Wasdale Head Inn

Other places of interest   *Hardknott Fort *(see p81)*, 15½ miles southeast, via Nether Wasdale, Santon Bridge, Eskdale Green and Dalegarth
*Muncaster Mill *(see p73)*, 11½ miles southwest on A595, via Nether Wasdale and Santon Bridge
*Muncaster Castle *(see p68)*, 12½ miles southwest — same route as for Muncaster Mill

 Ravenglass and Eskdale Railway car park, Ravenglass (west coast) ☎ (065 77) 278 (during season)

Hardknott Fort

The Romans called it *Mediobogdum* (which means 'situated in the middle of a curve' — and which refers to the contours of the Esk Valley at this point). Hardknott Fort was built during Emperor Hadrian's reign, AD117-138; (his name can be discerned, carved out of the masonry in the south gateway) and lies nine miles northeast of Ravenglass, facing Harknott Pass. Standing on a ledge, carved out of the hillside, 800ft above sea level, this three-acre fort was built to accommodate 500 men. Its function was the patrolling of the road which ran from Glannoventa Fort at Ravenglass on the west coast to Galava Fort at Ambleside. (Another road connected Galava Fort, the remains of which can be seen in a field next to Borran's Park at Waterhead in Ambleside, to Brougham at Penrith.) The position of the fort made it ideal for defence with near impossible access from the north and south and difficult approaches from the east, via Wrynose Pass and from the west (the coast). The original Roman road is completely buried and lies north (ie nearer the fort) of the present road.

The remains consist of the fort, the perimeter or curtain wall, which exceeds 5ft in height, the bases of four corner towers (from which the patrolling guard had a clear view on all sides), a detached bath house and a parade ground (the finest to survive in Great Britain), the latter of which is located a few hundred metres uphill from the east gate.

The centre of the fort pinpoints the location of the three principal administrative buildings; the headquarters or *principia*, which faced the *via Praetoria* (the road which ran up from the south gate to intercept the central road) was the administrative core of the fort; the Commander's house (*praetorium*) was located due west of the headquarters. Archaeological evidence from the 1960s indicated that this commander's house was never completed; the granary or *horreum* was for storing foods and supplies and was the largest building inside the fort. The Romans were sticklers for personal cleanliness. In between the south gate and Hardknott Pass itself are the remains of the bath house — or *balneum* — a rectangular

structure some 60ft long and 6½ft wide (18m×2m), which contained a stokehole at its west end and three rooms; a hot room or *caldarium*, a warm room or *tepidarium* and a dressing room or *apodyterium*. The latter contained a cold room or *frigidarium* and also a cold plunge bath. The *laconicum* was a rounded 'sweating bath' and its remains lie outside and at the eastern end of the main bath house.

The unfinished commander's house suggests that men could have been drafted from the fort to join with others, further north; this was initially to help with the building of Hadrian's Wall in AD122, and later for the invasion of Scotland and the building of the Antonine Wall, between the Firth and the Clyde, which subsequently undermined Hardknott's importance.

Hardknott offers the visitor superb views; west down Eskdale to the coast; east to the top of Hardknott Pass; south to Harter Fell and north, down a precipice to the Esk Valley and across to Scafell (3,163ft/964m) and Scafell Pike. The latter peak which rises 3,205ft (977m) above sea level, is the highest mountain in England.

The best view of Hardknott Fort itself is undoubtedly from the top of the pass. The Fort stands, isolated, in the middle ground like some large, drystone wall enclosure, with Eskdale snaking away, leading the eye to the coast and the Irish Sea in the background.

Hardknott Fort stands as a monument to the Roman's skill in building and strategic planning and is a 'must' for every Lakeland visitor.

Far left:
Hardknott Fort from the summit of Hardknott Pass.

Below left:
West side of the Fort wall and Fellstone foundations.

Below:
The commander's house.

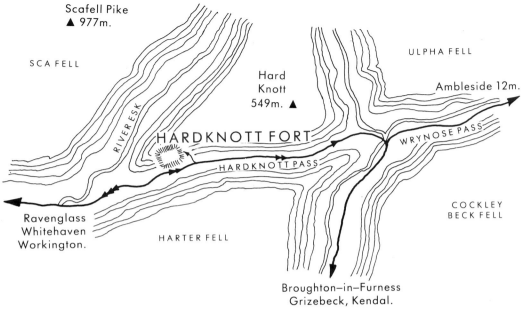

Scafell Pike
▲ 977m.

SCA FELL

ULPHA FELL

Hard
Knott
549m. ▲

Ambleside 12m.

RIVER ESK

HARDKNOTT FORT

HARDKNOTT PASS

WRYNOSE PASS

COCKLEY
BECK FELL

Ravenglass
Whitehaven
Workington.

HARTER FELL

Broughton—in—Furness
Grizebeck, Kendal.

Further information

Hardknott Fort   *OS Sheet 90, Ref NY 219015*
English Heritage Site

Location   9 miles northeast of Ravenglass, 12 miles southwest of Ambleside, facing Hardknott Pass

How to get there   From M6 Junction 36, A591 to Waterhead (just south of Ambleside). A593, then turn off A593 (signposts to Wrynose and Little Langdale), over Wrynose Pass, following the River Duddon, then over Hardknott Pass to the Fort
Note: *This route is unsuitable in winter/ unsuitable for coaches*

Alternative route   From M6 Junction 36, A590 via Newby Bridge to Greenodd, A5092, A595 following west coast to Muncaster Mill. About 1½ miles past the Mill, turn off A595 (signposts to Santon Bridge). At Santon Bridge follow signposts to Eskdale Green and then Hardknott Pass

Facilities   🚗; refreshments at Eskdale Green, Dalegarth; The Three Shires Inn at Little Langdale

Other places of interest
★Muncaster Castle *(see p68)*, 9 miles to the southwest
★Muncaster Mill *(see p73)*, 9 miles to the southwest
★Wasdale Head Church *(see p78)*, 15½ miles north, via Eskdale Green, Santon Bridge and Wastwater
★Galava Roman Fort (remains) *(see p89)*, 12 miles east at Waterhead, via Hardknott and Wrynose Passes and Little Langdale

Ravenglass and Eskdale Railway car park, Ravenglass (west coast) ☎ (065 77) 278 (during season)

Right:
The sweating bath.

'Townend' Troutbeck

Troutbeck is a small village, linear in plan, with houses dotted along a minor road which was formerly the main route over Kirkstone Pass from Windermere to Patterdale. Today the main A592 takes its place and by-passes the village to the east. The original mullioned windows of traditional oak may be seen in many of the old dwellings in Troutbeck, but of these houses it is the one called 'Townend', located towards the southern end of Troutbeck, which arouses most interest.

Townend was the family home of the Brownes for more than four centuries from 1525 when the first George Browne is recorded as having lived there, until 1943 when the daughter of the last George Browne died. In all, 12 generations of Brownes passed through Townend. The Brownes, a family with well established Troutbeck roots, were yeomen farmers, owning a number of tenements in the area and existing on the remuneration brought in from sheep farming. Some members of the family married into other yeoman families who were on a higher rung of the social ladder. One such marriage in 1623 took place between George Browne (great-grandson of the first George Browne) and Susannah Rawlinson of High Furness. In this year, the present house was constructed. Through the centuries the Brownes gradually branched from farming to different professions. George and Susannah's son, also called George, took up office as High Constable for the South Westmorland District and as such was responsible for raising the county's militia in the event of attack. His son, Benjamin, when appointed to the same position had to deal with James II's son, Prince James (the 'Old Pretender') when the aggressive Chevalier attacked from the north. Benjamin's younger son, Christopher, was a Kendal-based pharmacist. In 1735, he became mayor of Kendal. Another son, also called Benjamin, was a lawyer. Benjamin the lawyer, had a shortlived inheritance for he died just before his father in 1748. The legacy passed to the lawyer's son, George Browne, at seven, a mere infant. The infant George grew up to become a solicitor with a very large family. He had five daughters. One of

his three sons, a doctor practising in Ambleside, drowned in a sailing accident on Lake Windermere when he was only 20. The legacy was then passed down through two generations of eldest sons, both Georges, to the 10th and last George Browne (1834-1914). The Brownes were not only farmers, they were also craftsmen, and with their consummate skill they carved out fine oak pieces of furniture. The last George Browne was perhaps the most skilled of the Browne craftsmen — many examples of his and other Browne family pieces of furniture can be found throughout the house. The last

Below:
The firehouse.

Above:
Townend.

George Browne kept all the old documents, books, household paraphernalia and furniture collected by his ancestors. Townend has every copy of the *Westmorland Gazette* since it was first introduced in 1818 when Thomas de Quincey (a friend of the poet William Wordsworth), famous for his 'Confessions of an English Opium Eater', was editor. George Browne's daughter, Clara Jane, was bequeathed the estates in 1914. When she died in 1943 Townend passed to her cousin who died in 1945. Two years later the National Trust acquired Townend together with some 800 acres of land.

The home is very well preserved — a unique example of a 17th century Lakeland statesman's dwelling. Apart from the typical slate roof, the exterior is noted for its four large round chimneys and mullioned windows of oak. Opposite the main dwelling are the old farm buildings, one of which, like so many others in Troutbeck, houses a spinning gallery.

Various alterations over the centuries have resulted in confusion to the extent that many parts of the building cannot be accurately dated. The main part of the house is split into two: the accommodation area or 'fire-house'

Above left:
The main bedroom. The bed bears the initials of George and Ellinor Browne, and the date '1686'. To compensate for the slope of the floor, the legs of the bed are longer on one side than the other.

Above:
The kitchen or 'down-house'.

and the kitchen or 'down-house'. The fire-house — one large room — is believed to be the oldest section, dating from about the turn of the 17th century. The kitchen probably dates from 1623, which would coincide with the marriage of Susannah Rawlinson and George Browne. The marriage contract stipulated that George Browne had to carry out extensive rebuilding at Townend. When the kitchen was added, a passage called the 'hallan' was created between the fire-house and kitchen, which connected the two. The front entrance led into the hallan. At some time before 1800, a new entrance was made in the fire-house and the old hallan entrance was replaced with a window; the hallan itself was converted into a pantry. In about 1672 a north wing was constructed which houses the library (formerly the parlour) and the state bedroom; the date '1672' can be seen on the bed. The west wing, which today provides accommodation for the curator, probably dates from 1739 and the time of Benjamin Browne (the lawyer) and his second wife, Elizabeth Longmire. In Victorian times, fireplaces were added and other items of furniture introduced. With the exception of the building of a porch in 1912 and the insertion of the library's bay window in 1905, there have been no alterations in the 20th century.

The old kitchen or down-house (c1623) has an early 19th century iron grating which replaced the original open hearth. The kitchen shelves display many now defunct utensils. Some of the panels on the cupboard doors were skilfully worked by the last George Browne.

The fire-house (circa late 16th century) has its original oak mullioned windows, typically set low down. The large Gothic-style chimneypiece is Victorian. Crafted in the 17th century, the huge oak table is too big to have been brought in from outside and was almost certainly built in situ. Another fine carving is on show here — a spinning wheel crafted by the last George Browne in 1893 for his daughter, Lucy Eleanor. The library, its shelves stocked with many books covering a variety of topics from English literature to medicine, farming to housing, was formerly the parlour in the 17th century. The Kidderminster carpet is reputed to have been the work of Troutbeck weavers and dates from c1750.

The state bedroom was originally built as two separate rooms. Today it exhibits some fine carved panels crafted by the last George Browne; the bed, complete with canopy (an old-fashioned draught excluder), in the main bedroom bears George and Ellinor Browne's initials and the year '1686'. The legs of the bed on one side are shorter to allow for the gradient of the floor. By the staircase and in the kitchen are two very fine long case clocks, dating from c1750.

Seemingly frozen by time, the interior evokes an atmosphere of a bygone lifestyle of the yeoman family, which has now all but vanished. Townend is a document of one particular type of family's existence and is cared for by The National Trust so that today's and future generations may gain knowledge and seek to understand an important chapter of Lakeland's heritage.

Further information

Townend, Troutbeck *OS Sheet 90, Ref NY 407026*
National Trust Site ☎*(096 63) 32628*

Further enquiries	National Trust Regional Office, Rothay Holme, Rothay Road, Ambleside, Cumbria LA22 0EJ
Location	At the southern end of Troutbeck, about 3½ miles southeast of Ambleside
How to get there	From M6 Junction 36, A591 to Windermere, follow signs to Ambleside. Turn off the A591 at Troutbeck Bridge. Townend is signposted **Note:** *Roads leading to Townend and Troutbeck are unsuitable for coaches*

Admission charged

Opening times	Easter-end of October, every day except Saturdays and Mondays (Open Bank Holiday Mondays) 2pm-6pm (or dusk if earlier)
Facilities	🚗; **WC**; refreshments at Windermere and Ambleside
Other places of interest	★Galava Roman Fort (remains) *(see p89)*, Borrans Road, Waterhead, South of Ambleside ★Bridge House *(see p90)*, in Rydal Road, Ambleside, on main A591 to Grasmere and Keswick ★Belle Isle — A5074 from Windermere to Bowness-on-Windermere, then ferry to Belle Isle

 Victoria Street, Windermere
☎ (096 62) 6499

Galava Roman Fort, Waterhead (Ambleside)

At Waterhead, just south of Ambleside, where the waters of the Brathay and Rothay flow into Lake Windermere, traces of the Roman Fort of Galava may be seen in a field, adjacent to Borrans Park, which is today owned by the National Trust, although the remains are in the hands of English Heritage. The Celtic name of Galava is thought to mean 'rigorous stream'. The fort dates from around AD79; it was originally built of wood and turf to hold about 200 men. It was restructured during the early part of the 2nd century, during Emperor Hadrian's reign (117-138). This second and much larger fort, built of stone and encompassed by timber outer buildings, could accommodate a garrison of nearer 500 men. The fort was one of several defences built to control the road which ran from the coastal fort of Glannoventa at Ravenglass, up Hardknott Pass to Mediobogdum (Hardknott Fort) and then over Wrynose Pass down into Little Langdale and thence to Ambleside. Another road linked Ambleside with Brocavum fort at Brougham (Penrith), via High Street (Brete Street) and High Raise. At Galava, archaeologists have uncovered the foundations of two gateways and two corner towers. Inside the fort, the remains of the headquarters, the commander's house and granaries may be seen.

Below:
Remains of the granaries (*Horrea*) at Galava Fort, Waterhead.

Bridge House, Ambleside

Nearly one mile north of Galava Fort is the town of Ambleside. This once strategically important town (at the junction of the old Roman Roads which ran from Ambleside to Ravenglass, on the west coast, and Ambleside to Brougham at Penrith) which observes a rush-bearing ceremony every year on the first Saturday in July, has one of the most famous and recognisable sites in the Lake District. It is, of course, Bridge House which the visitor will see at the northern end of town in Rydal Road. This small building, on a slight incline which straddles Stock Beck, has only two rooms one on top of the other — and is linked by an external staircase. At the back of this tiny building one can discern the remains of a doorway. The house was one of many buildings owned by the influential Braithwaite family of Ambleside Hall (Ambleside Hall used to be in nearby Smithy Brow). In 1494, Richard Braithwaite was the first of such name recorded as living at the Hall. Bridge House was probably built in the early years of the 16th century as a means of providing access to the field on the other side of Stock Beck.

As the 18th century progressed, Bridge House became surrounded by a variety of mills (corn mills, weaving mills, bark mills), all utilising the water from the beck, which would drive the waterwheels and which would in turn power the milling machinery. The combined noise from the waterwheels and machinery must have been quite overpowering — an infernal din to the passing stranger! In the mills' heyday, it was thought that Bridge House may have served as the local counting house. In his guide of 1819, resident artist William Green noted that Bridge House was used as a tea room-cum-weaver's shop. Bridge House has seen many different uses from an apple store to a summer house. In 1905, a local cobbler used the ground floor as his workshop.

A fine etching by William Green, published in May 1821, shows the house surrounded by unspoiled woodland before the construction, in 1843, of Rydal Road (which today is the main A591 out of Ambleside to Grasmere and Keswick). In 1953, tempestuous weather brought flooding to many homes in Ambleside. As water cascaded down Stock Ghyll, the level of the tiny beck rose dramatically and peaked — not quite reaching the top of the Bridge House arch; however, the little house and its underlying structure remained sound.

This quaint little building was bought by a handful of locals in 1926 for £450 and given to the National Trust. Since 1956, Bridge House has been a National Trust Information Centre. This small, seemingly toy-like building, has attracted photographers, artists, historians and other inquisitive folk for generations.

Further information

Bridge House, Ambleside   *OS Sheet 90,*
Ref NY 376047
National Trust Information Centre

Galava Roman Fort (remains)   *OS Sheet 90,*
Ref NY 373034
National Trust site

Enquiries	National Trust Regional Office, Rothay Holme, Rothay Road, Ambleside, Cumbria LA22 0EJ ☎(05394) 33883
Location	*Bridge House* — at the northern end of the town. Bridge House straddles Stock Beck in Rydal Road *Galava Roman Fort (remains)* — 1 mile south of Bridge House, in a field next to Borrans Park, at Waterhead
How to get there	*Bridge House* — From M6 Junction 36, A591 to Windermere and then on to Ambleside. At the top of Compston Road bear left following A591 (signs to Grasmere and Keswick). Bridge House is on the left *Galava Roman Fort* — A591 from Windermere, turn off at Waterhead (A593). Car park at Waterhead is 200yd (183m) from the remains of the fort

Opening times	Bridge House, daily Easter-end October, 10am-5pm. Galava Fort, daily, all year round
Facilities	🚗; For Bridge House use the Rydal Road car park; for Galava use the Waterhead car park **WC** ; Rydal Road car park and Waterhead; refreshments at Ambleside
Other places of interest	★Brockhole, The Lake District National Park Visitor Centre, midway between Windermere and Ambleside on the A591 ★Rydal Mount (and Dora's Field) between Ambleside and Grasmere, turn off A591 at Rydal Church *(see p93)* ★Dove Cottage, follow A591 out of Ambleside to Grasmere *(see p97)*

(1) Old Courthouse, Church Street, Ambleside
☎ (05394) 32602
(2) Waterhead car park on Borrans Road
☎(05394) 32729 (during season)

Above:
Bridge House — the ground floor shop, part of The National Trust Information Centre.

Far left:
Bridge House.

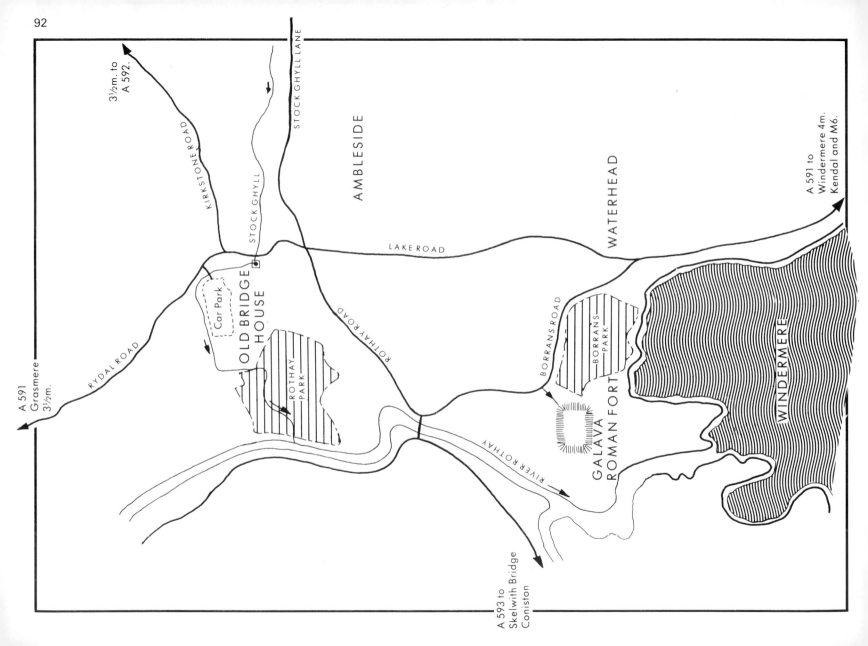

3½m. to A 592.

KIRKSTONE ROAD

STOCK GHYLL

STOCK GHYLL LANE

AMBLESIDE

WATERHEAD

A 591 to Windermere 4m. Kendal and M6.

LAKE ROAD

A 591 Grasmere 3½m.

RYDAL ROAD

Car Park

OLD BRIDGE HOUSE

ROTHAY ROAD

ROTHAY PARK

BORRANS ROAD

BORRANS PARK

GALAVA ROMAN FORT

RIVER ROTHAY

WINDERMERE

A 593 to Skelwith Bridge Coniston

Rydal Mount

'Rydal Mount is the nicest place in the world for children', once wrote Dorothy Wordsworth. Rydal Mount was the last home of William Wordsworth before his death in 1850. The house is situated between Grasmere and Ambleside on a road off the main A591, a little way up from Rydal Church. The original road (the 'coffin track') from Ambleside to Grasmere runs behind the house.

Rydal Mount was built in the mid-16th century, and in 1574 parish records indicate that one John Keene owned this yeoman farmhouse, which he called 'Keenes'. The Keene family were followed by the Walkers, and around the turn of the 18th century the Knott family from Grasmere bought the house. Keenes remained in the Knott's possession for a century until 1803 when a Liverpudlian named Mr Ford North purchased the house for £2,500 and subsequently renamed it 'Rydal Mount'. Lady Diana le Fleming of neighbouring Rydal Hall bought Rydal Mount in 1812.

William Wordsworth and his family were, at this time, living at the Old Parsonage in Grasmere, having moved out of Allan Bank due to smoking chimneys. In that year of 1812, William and Mary Wordsworth lost two of their children — Catherine and Thomas aged three and six respectively — and so the village which had once enticed the great poet 'on nature's invitation', now forced him to leave on pain of grief. In May 1813, William Wordsworth with his wife Mary — 'A perfect woman, nobly plann'd' — children Dora, John and William, sister Dorothy and Mary's sister Sara Hutchinson, moved to Rydal Mount which they rented from the le Fleming family and here they lived for the rest of their lives. In their first year here, William was made 'Distributor of Stamps' for Westmorland County, a post which carried a generous remuneration.

In the dining room below the spice cupboard is a chair which once belonged to the poet. The spice cupboard itself was crafted by Edward Knott and bears the date, '1710'. Edward's son, Michael, carried out alterations at Rydal Mount in the mid-18th century. The yew candlesticks on the table were made in 1895 by the joiner

Edward Wilson, from the tree which William Wordsworth originally planted in the churchyard at Grasmere and which was felled in 1891. Up until 1968 the library and drawing room were two separate rooms. The enlarged drawing room is therefore a relatively modern feature. On the east wall (library end) over the fireplace hangs the only known painting of Dorothy Wordsworth. The portrait by S. Crosthwaite was painted in 1833 when 'Wordsworth's exquisite sister' was 62 years old. On the opposite wall is Henry Inman's fine portrait of William Wordsworth painted in 1844. Wordsworth took over as Poet Laureate from Southey who died in March of the previous year. Inman painted two identical portraits of the new Poet Laureate: the one painted for Mary Wordsworth is seen here and the other twin hangs in Pennsylvania University. A glass cabinet near Wordsworth's sofa contains many of the poet's belongings which include his prayer book, rush light holder and ink stand. It is difficult to realise in our present age of television, video and radio, that in the poet's day they had none of these luxuries and would pass the time away by dancing, partying and by reading extracts from their journals. In the closing years of the 18th century, Dorothy

Above:
Dora's bedroom.

began to write her journals, starting from the times spent at Grasmere. In 1874 Dorothy's accounts were finally published — nearly 20 years after her death. On hearing an account of their walk together along the shores of Ullswater from his sister's journals, dated 15 April 1802, nearly two years after the event, the poet was inspired to write the famous lines:

I wandered lonely as a cloud
That floats on high o'er vales and hills
When all at once I saw a crowd
A host of golden daffodils.

Above the stairs is a large portrait of the poet's brother-in-law, Thomas Hutchinson. William and Mary's bedroom houses portraits of Queen Victoria and Edward, Prince of Wales, which were given to the poet personally by the great queen when William Wordsworth was created Poet Laureate. Dora was undoubtedly the poet's favourite child. She used to accompany her father on many a trip. Despite contracting tuberculosis when she was only 18, Dora was determined to get on with her life. In 1841 she married Edward Quillinan (whose portrait hangs above her bed) who had retired as an officer in the Irish Dragoons. The marriage at Bath came at a time when her health was rapidly deteriorating. Six years later she finally relinquished her struggle with a disease which claimed so many a life. A melancholy poet, overburdened with grief in the latter stages of his life declared: 'She is ever with me and will be to the last moment of my life'.

On the top floor of the house is Wordsworth's study, which he added in around 1838. The room is full of first editions of the poet's works, displayed in glass cases. John Wordsworth, the poet's brother, was killed when the ship of which he was captain, *The Earl of Abergavenny*, foundered on the rocks during a storm off Portland Bill. His sword may be seen in the study. We also learn that a nephew of the poet, Charles Wordsworth, whilst studying at Oxford, organised the first Oxford and Cambridge boat race in 1829. The Oxford crew won! There is a dramatic layout of the four-and-a-half acre garden which William Wordsworth created to

his own designs. He restructured the sloping terrace, which leads up to the summer house (a spot which commands a beautiful view of Rydal Water) and along which he would walk up and down, composing lines of verse, 'through the vicissitudes of many a year'. In his latter years at Rydal Mount, a grief stricken bard found that his 'spontaneous overflow of powerful feelings' were not so often forthcoming. Once in a while he would deliver poetry to match his youthful brilliance such as the 1835 composition 'Extempore Effusion upon the Death of James Hogg', in which he reflects on the loss of friends and loved ones:

How fast has brother followed brother,
From sunshine to the sunless land!
A timid voice, that asks in whispers
'Who next will drop and disappear?'.

Above:
The dining room.

Far left:
Rydal Mount.

A level terrace was built below the sloping terrace and a far terrace was excavated beyond the summer house. It was the poet's belief that any garden should be informal, that it should blend in with its surroundings, and that it should have 'lawn and trees and carefully planted so as not to obscure the view'.

After Dora's passing in 1847, William Wordsworth went down to the small field (which lies between the house and the main A591) which he had purchased for £300, and together with his wife, sister and gardener, James Dixon, they got down on their hands and knees and planted hundreds of daffodils there as a memorial to beloved Dora: 'I never saw daffodils so beautiful'. Two years before his death in 1935, the poet's grandson, Gordon Wordsworth, gave Dora's Field to the National Trust. Every Easter, the field is alive with a multitude of yellow heads nodding in the breeze.

In 1850 the great poet died at Rydal Mount. He was 80 years old. Sister Dorothy died in 1855 followed by the poet's wife Mary in 1859. William Wordsworth left behind 70,000 lines of verse, 40,000 more than any other poet! The house has been open to the public since 1970, for 'I often ask myself what will become of Rydal Mount after our day'.

Further information

Rydal Mount   *OS Sheet 90, Ref NY 364064*

Enquiries	Rydal Mount, Rydal, Ambleside, Cumbria ☎(05394) 33002
Location	Just over 2 miles southeast of Grasmere, 1½ miles northwest of Ambleside, up Rydal Hill (off A591)
How to get there	From M6 Junction 36, follow A591 to Windermere, then on to Ambleside, following signs to Grasmere and Keswick. Turn off (signposted) at Rydal Church. Rydal Mount is a little way up the hill, on the left **Note:** *Dora's Field (National Trust) can be reached via Rydal Churchyard*

Admission charged

Opening times	1 March-31 October: house and gardens open every day 9.30am-5pm; 1 November-end February: 10am-4pm. Closed on Tuesdays
Facilities	🚗; **WC**; refreshments at Ambleside/Grasmere
Other places of interest	★Dove Cottage (see p97), just over 2 miles to the northwest, off A591 ★Bridge House (see p90), 1½ miles southeast on A591 in Ambleside ★Galava Roman Fort (remains) (see p89), 2½ miles south at Waterhead

(1) Old Courthouse, Church Street, Ambleside ☎ (05394) 32602
(2) Red Bank Road, Grasmere ☎ (096 65) 245 (during season)

RYDAL FELL

RYDAL BECK

SCANDALE FELL

Grasmere 2½m.
Keswick 16m.

A 591

RYDAL MOUNT

RYDAL WATER

DORA'S FIELD (NT)

RYDAL HALL

LOUGHRIGG FELL

A 591

Ambleside 2m.
Windermere 6½m.

Dove Cottage, Grasmere

Just off the main A591 route from Ambleside to Keswick, at Grasmere, is a row of cottages which were collectively known as Town End, prior to the construction of the main road in the 1830s. One of these dwellings used to be an inn called 'The Dove and Olive Bough' which offered many 'a greeting of good ale'. After the great poet William Wordsworth and his family lived here, the house was named 'Dove Cottage'. Building of this limewashed cottage with its slate roof dates from around the beginning of the 17th century.

Wordsworth and his sister Dorothy moved into their tiny abode in 1799, five days before Christmas. The poet married Mary Hutchinson in 1802, for 'she was a phantom of delight, when first she gleam'd upon my sight'. In the ensuing years, the first three children — John, Dora and Thomas — were born.

The interior is still very much as it was during the Wordworths' nine-year occupancy, with most of the original furniture surviving. When you step through the front door, you will find yourself in the kitchen, which served the dual purpose of kitchen and living area. Next to this room is the actual kitchen where the food was prepared and the washing was carried out. A little room in one corner of the kitchen was used as a larder. A small stream running underneath the floor was a firm guarantee that the room would be kept cool, and the food fresh.

On the half-landing there is a door (inserted in 1804) which opens out into the lovely hilly gardens. Upstairs and positioned directly over the kitchen is the main sitting room where the Wordsworths entertained many friends, like Samuel Taylor Coleridge (who used to sojourn from his home, Greta Hall, in Keswick) and Walter Scott. Here, too, Wordsworth wrote many of his outstanding works (which include his autobiography entitled *The Prelude*, finished in 1805, and two volumes of short poems which include *Daffodils*, *To the Cuckoo*, and *Immortality Ode*) often amidst constant distractions of the hustle and bustle of family and visitors coming and

going. This won him the admiration of his sister Dorothy, who wondered how such glittering work could be so forthcoming from a man surrounded by potentially exasperating confusion.

Wordsworth's portrait (1806) by Henry Edridge, hangs over the fireplace. There are three embroidered seats, worked by Dora Wordsworth, Edith Southey and Sara Coleridge. The poet's chair, of special design, enabled him to write on something solid when there was no desk

Below:
Wordsworth's sitting room.

to hand. The Wordsworths loved their garden and over the years planted an array of shrubs and flowers. They built a summer house lined with moss, between 1804 and 1805. The poet described the garden in *A Farewell* (1802) as 'thou little nook of mountain ground'.

As the family grew in size, and the frequency with which friends would visit also increased, it was clear that Dove Cottage was now too small for their needs. Indeed, Dorothy noted in her journal of March 1806 that 'we are crammed into our little nest, edge-full'. So in 1808 the Wordsworths moved to a much larger house called Allan Bank, just west of the centre of Grasmere Village. They spent three years here, followed by a brief spell at the Old Parsonage, before moving to their final house, Rydal Mount (a few miles away) in May 1813.

Another friend of the family, Thomas De Quincey, famed for his *The Confessions of an English Opium Eater* and *Recollection of the Lakes and Lake Poets*, moved into Dove Cottage on the Wordsworth's departure. Thomas De Quincey owned the property for 18 years. The years 1836-90 saw a variety of tenants come and go. In 1890 a trust was formed for the preservation of Dove Cottage. The poet, his wife Mary, sister Dorothy and daughter Dora, are buried in the graveyard of Grasmere's St Oswald's Church.

The daily routine of housework and garden chores, the relatively basic lifestyle of a family in a tranquil and picturesque Lakeland village, coupled with a steady flow of brilliant poetry, epitomised William Wordsworth's idea of 'plain living and high thinking'.

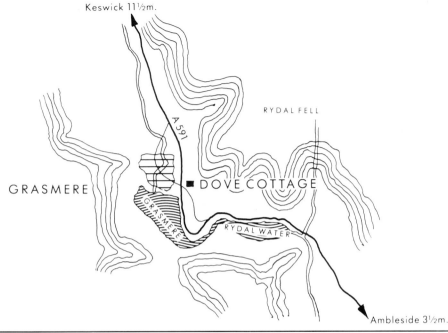

Keswick 11½m.

A 591

RYDAL FELL

GRASMERE

■ DOVE COTTAGE

GRASMERE

RYDAL WATER

Ambleside 3½m.

Above right:
The grave of William and Mary Wordsworth at St Oswald's Church, Grasmere.

Further information

Dove Cottage   *OS Sheet 90, Ref NY 343069*

Enquiries	The Wordsworth Trust, Dove Cottage, Grasmere, Cumbria LA22 9SH ☎ (09665) 544/547
Location	3½ miles northwest of Ambleside, just off A591 at Grasmere
How to get there	M6 Junction 36, A591 to Windermere, Ambleside — thence to Grasmere

Admission charged

Opening times	Daily from 9.30am to 5.30pm

Facilities	🚗; 🚌; **WC** ; restaurant; book/gift shop (Wordsworth Museum next door). Additional facilities in the centre of Grasmere
Other places of interest	★Rydal Mount *(see p93)*, just over 2 miles southeast (off A591) ★Bridge House, Ambleside *(see p90)*, 3½ miles to the southeast, via A591 ★Galava Roman Fort (remains) *(see p89)*, 4 miles to the southeast, at Waterhead ★Brockhole, The Lake District National Park Visitor Centre, on A591 between Windermere and Ambleside

 Red Bank Road, Grasmere ☎ (096 65) 245 24hr information line ☎ (09665) 580 (during season)

Wordsworth House, Cockermouth

In northwest Cumbria, where the River Cocker merges with the River Derwent, is the market town of Cockermouth. John Dalton — well remembered for his atomic theory — was born here, so too was the ringleader of the *Bounty* mutineers, Fletcher Christian. But the town is undoubtedly best known as being the birthplace of that great Lakeland bard, William Wordsworth.

The second son of John and Ann Wordsworth, William was born on 7 April 1770 — followed by his sister Dorothy a year later, and brothers John and Christopher in the ensuing years — in that large Georgian building whose front façade dominates the town's main street. Wordsworth House, which backs on to the River Derwent, was built in 1745 for the Sheriff of Cumberland, Joshua Lucock. The Lowthers acquired the house a couple of years later and Sir James Lowther subsequently let it to his attorney, the poet's father.

Much of Wordsworth's early childhood at the house was spent in the company of his beloved sister Dorothy, playing by the river, lapping up the sun in the warm summer months, or exploring the nearby ruins of the 12th century castle. It was during these years that a very special brother-sister relationship was kindled which was to last until the very end. William and Dorothy became inseparable — the best of friends — who truly valued each other's company. Dorothy was the constant influence in his life; her incessant drive and devotion helped to provide the inspiration with which his literary talent could be unleashed, enabling him to deliver upon society an anthology of poems with such eloquence. Fond childhood memories of Cockermouth — so close to his heart — the poet was to relate many a time throughout his 80-year life, but on one occasion in particular during his final year of bachelorhood at Dove Cottage in Grasmere, Wordsworth wrote *The Sparrow's Nest* in 1801. In this poem he not only remembers their favourite haunt — the bottom of the garden, where many a bird would build a nest amidst 'a thick hedge of privet

and roses . . .' but also remembers the inspiration and affection which his dear sister gave him, for 'she gave me eyes, she gave me ears . . . and love, and thought, and joy'. These good times of his boyhood years were marred with the untimely death of his mother in 1778. His father passed away in 1783, finally unlocking the heavy burden of five grief-stricken years. This was indeed a traumatic time for the young William Wordsworth, as he stood by the graveside, a mere lad of 13 years, tossing his tribute of boxwood on to the coffin and waving his dear father goodbye for the very last time. In the aftermath of the funeral, William and Dorothy were to spend nearly a decade apart. William, and his two younger brothers together with older brother Richard, were looked after by their grandparents in Penrith and Dorothy went to stay with relatives in Halifax.

In later years, the poet was to return to his native town with increased frequency. In 1836 he put forward a plan for the construction of a new church. A commemorative fountain was built in the town in 1896 in Wordsworth's name. Wordsworth House was very nearly demolished, but rescued by money raised by public subscription and handed over to the NT who have gradually restored and furnished it with items from the period, including some Wordsworth items.

The house has undergone various programmes of alteration over the years, but it still features a lot of the original panelling, for example as seen in the drawing room and parlour. The fireplaces in these two rooms are also original. Portraits hanging in the dining room now take the place of the Georgian panelling. In this room, too, is a fine Broadwood piano with a mahogany casing; the drawing room houses an old grand piano — another Broadwood which is finished in rosewood. Both pianos date from 1815. The library houses two of the poet's

Far left:
Wordsworth house.

Below left:
Dorothy Wordsworth's tripod table in the bedroom.

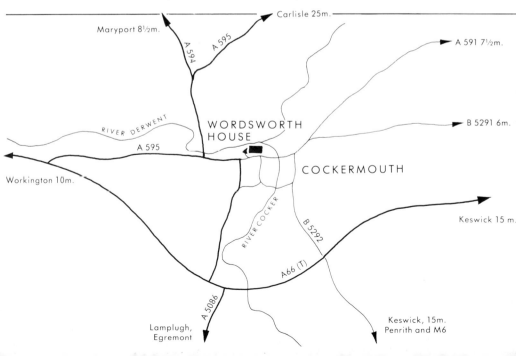

bookcases, one of which was brought in from Rydal Mount. A portrait of Wordsworth, hanging over the fireplace, was completed after his death. In the bedroom the four poster bed — a Hepplewhite — was brought into the house at a later stage and dates from around 1770. Dorothy Wordsworth's tripod table and oval mirror were brought in from Allan Bank — the Wordsworths' home from 1808-11. This lovely Georgian dwelling also contains some fine pieces of quality china.

Wordsworth House has been under the protection of the National Trust since 1939 and serves as a memorial to the great Poet Laureate.

Further information

Wordsworth House, Cockermouth *OS Sheet 89, Ref NY 118301*
National Trust Site

Enquiries	Wordsworth House, Main Street, Cockermouth, Cumbria ☎ (0900) 824805
Location	Main Street in Cockermouth, northwest Cumbria. The River Derwent runs behind the house
How to get there	From M6 Junction 40, A66 (west), via Keswick, Bassenthwaite Lake, then turn off on to the A5086. Wordsworth House is well signposted from A66/A5086 junction into Cockermouth

Admission charged

Opening times	Good Friday-5 November, every day except Thursday 11am-5pm; Sunday 2pm-5pm
Facilities	🚗 in the town; **WC** ; small café and shop
Other places of interest	⋆Castlerigg Stone Circle *(see p104)*, 17 miles southeast. A66 via Bassenthwaite Lake and Keswick

 Riverside car park, Market Street, Cockermouth, Cumbria ☎ (0900) 822634 (during season)

Castlerigg Stone Circle, Keswick

Castlerigg Stone Circle is without a doubt the Lake District's most well known (although not the largest) stone circle. The formation of stones lies in a field on high ground, two miles from Keswick and the northern end of Derwent Water.

Stone circles such as this and Penrith's Long Meg and Her Daughters date from the late Neolithic/early Bronze Age period (c1000BC). The total count of stones here is 38 and most of these are still standing. The circle measures just over 100ft (30.5m) in diameter and contains a small inner-rectangle of 10 stones.

One can only guess as to the purpose of such circles. Nobody really knows whether they fulfilled a religious or sacrificial function. Some have suggested that Castlerigg and other circles were forms of Neolithic time calculators. Other schools of thought suggest that these sites were used as ancient burial grounds, but whatever their function, it is incredible to think that Neolithic/Bronze Age man possessed the means by which he could shift huge blocks of stone from one place to another.

The mood at Castlerigg is constantly changing, whether the stones are viewed on a hot summer's day or on a windswept winter's day with rain lashing down over the fells. Keats came here on a stormy day in 1818. The dark clouds loured over this site and he later recounted his visit in *Hyperion II*.

Left:
Rectangle of 10 stones contained within the circle.

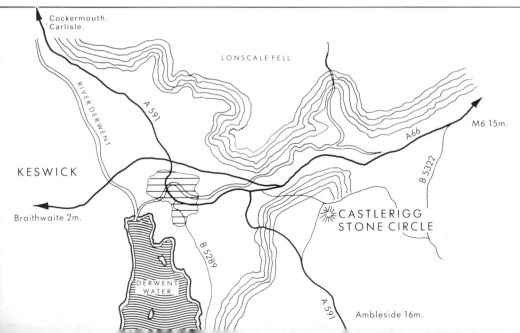

Further information

Castlerigg Stone Circle   *OS Sheet 90, Ref NY 293236*
National Trust and English Heritage site

Location	2 miles east of Keswick
How to get there	M6 Junction 40, A66 following signs to Keswick, turn off A66 on to minor road. Stone circle is signposted
Facilities	🚗; refreshments and **WC** in Keswick
Other places of interest	★Wordsworth House, Cockermouth — 17 miles northwest, via A66

 Moot Hall, Market Square, Keswick
☎ (0596) 72645

Northeast Lakeland

Dalemain

Three miles south of Penrith and just north of Ullswater is the Hasell (pronounced 'Hazel') family home. 'Dalemain' is derived from the Saxon 'Mani's Valley', and a settlement has existed here since these times. From the 14th century it was owned by the Leyton family until 1689, when Sir Edward Hasell (secretary to the Countess of Pembroke, Lady Anne Clifford) bought the house for £2,710, and it has remained in the Hasell family ever since. A defensive pele tower, in the west range, was constructed here in the 12th century. John de Morville owned the tower at this time and his brother Hugh was one of four men who, on misinterpreting Henry II's words, subsequently murdered Archbishop Thomas à Becket in Canterbury Cathedral in 1172. After this outrage, Hugh was temporarily hidden in the tower.

A hall was then built on to the tower, which was thus converted into a manor house. During Elizabeth I's reign two wings were added, one each side of the hall. The present Georgian building of pink sandstone ashlar was completed in around 1750 by the second Edward ('Blackcap') Hasell, so-called because he always donned a black cap whilst hunting. Edward improved the Longhorn breed of cattle, which were the foundation stock for many of the current breeds found throughout Britain today. Blackcap's son, Williams (Williams was the maiden name of Sir Edward Hasell's wife, Dorothy) was responsible for the layout of the surrounding woodlands and it was this job which gained him the nickname of 'The Planter'. Since Blackcap's alterations to the building and the Planter's layout of the woodlands, the estate has remained essentially unchanged.

The use of oak features throughout the house, from the panelling in the drawing room and old oak room, through to the dining room and fine staircase. The Chinese drawing room is noted for its hand-painted wallpaper and carved rococo chimneypiece. The dining room houses a folding screen which was brought over from India's Coromandel coast in the 17th century. The ceiling of the Fretwork Room on the first floor of the

Right:
The Chinese drawing room.

Centre right:
The fretwork room on the first floor of the tower. Dating from the mid 16th century, the ceiling is of fretwork plaster.

Far right:
Queen Anne walnut escritoire in the Chinese drawing room.

tower is of fretwork plaster and dates from around 1550; it is decorated with, among other designs, Tudor roses. The base of the tower today houses the Westmorland and Cumberland Yeomanry Museum.

During your tour of Dalemain, look out for the priest's hiding hole, located behind the store cupboard in the work-room. There are many family portraits around the house, including masterpieces by Van Dyke. The Hasell family crest, a squirrel, may be seen engraved on the dining room table's silverware.

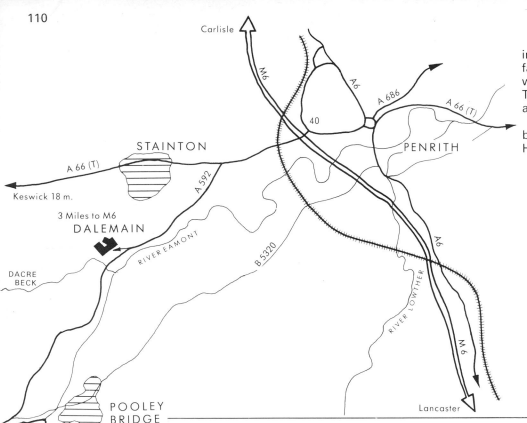

During the troubled times of the border wars, a small inner courtyard was built next to the pele tower. The farm buildings which form the present 'outer' courtyard would have been built after such conflict had subsided. The 16th century great barn houses a museum of defunct agricultural and household paraphernalia.

This delightful Georgian residence, surrounded by beautiful gardens, is currently owned by Mrs Sylvia (née Hasell) McCosh and her husband, Bryce McCosh.

Further information

Dalemain   *OS Sheet 90, Ref NY 478269*

Enquiries   Dalemain, Penrith, Cumbria CA11 0HB
☎ (085 36) 450

Location   3 miles southwest of Penrith on the A592, 2½ miles northeast of Pooley Bridge

How to get there   M6 Junction 40, A66 (signposts to Keswick) then A592

Admission charged

Opening times   Easter-October, every day except Fridays and Saturdays, 11.15am-5pm

Facilities   🚗; **WC**; restaurant and gift shop

Other places of interest   ★St Michael's Church, Barton *(see p111)*, southeast on B5320 out of Pooley Bridge
★Brougham Castle *(see p115)*, 4 miles via A592, A66 (east bound)

(1) Eusemere car park, Pooley Bridge, Cumbria ☎ (085 36) 530
(2) Robinson's School, Middlegate, Penrith, Cumbria ☎ (0768) 67466 (during season)

St Michael's Church, Barton

The parish church of St Michael, Barton, lies 1½ miles north of Pooley Bridge and southwest of Penrith on a site which may have prehistoric origins. The Norman style building of nave, chancel and tower can be dated to the mid-12th century.

Standing at the back, or western end, of the church, the north aisle of 1280 is on the left and the south aisle of 1250 is on the right. The centre aisle leads the visitor's eye to the most notable feature of the church, the tower's double-rounded arch, believed to be Augustinian and later widened in 1330. The aisle continues to the chancel. The stonework surrounds of the east window are early 14th century, but the stained glass only dates back to 1913. The Bishop's chair and panelling behind the altar and Communion rails are all late 17th century.

Richard Wordsworth, the great Lakeland poet's grandfather (a Yorkshireman, born in 1680) was laid to rest beneath the chancel in 1760. He was reputed to be the area's first Wordsworth. A stone in the chancel is dedicated to the memory of William Wordsworth's aunt, Anne Myers, who married the curate of Barton and headmaster of the local grammar school, the Rev Thomas Myers, in 1763. At the time of her death in 1787, her son John was studying at Cambridge with William and it was whilst touring the Lakes with John and friend, Samuel Taylor Coleridge, that William decided to settle in Grasmere.

To the north of the chancel, on the floor, is a tombstone which bears a cross, sword and shield of Lancaster, thought to be early 14th century. An archway in the south wall of the chancel provides access to the Lancaster Chapel. Over the centuries this small chapel has seen a variety of different uses, from a chantry to a burial site, until its restoration in 1956. Part of a 13th century priest's door may be seen to the east of the chapel's entrance arch. On the chapel wall are three memorial stones, dedicated to John Wordsworth (William's cousin and contemporary at Cambridge) and to John's two wives, Anne and Elisabeth. Anne died in

112

Previous page:
St Michael's church, Barton.

1815 and is buried here, but Elisabeth is buried at Walton, Liverpool.

The font is around 700 years old. The entrance porch was built by Moses Sisson in the late 17th century; on the upper step you can just discern the initials 'M.S.'. A splendid lych gate serves as a memorial to those who fell in the two world wars.

Right:
The east window.

Centre right:
The nave, showing the tower's double rounded arch.

Far right:
Lest we forget: the lych gate commemorates those who died in two world wars.

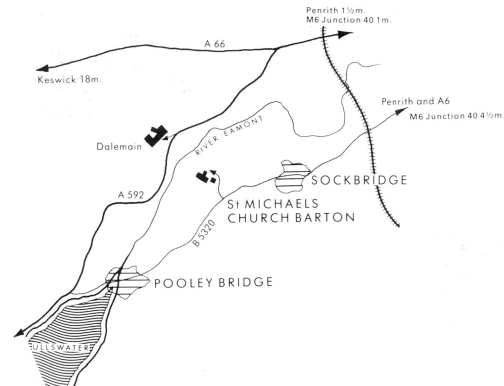

Keswick 18m.

A 66

Penrith 1½m.
M6 Junction 40 1m.

Penrith and A6
M6 Junction 40 4½m.

Dalemain

RIVER EAMONT

A 592

B 5320

SOCKBRIDGE

St MICHAELS
CHURCH BARTON

POOLEY BRIDGE

ULLSWATER

Above:
**Located to the north of the chancel, this tombstone
bears the cross, sword and shield of Lancaster.**

Further information

Barton, St Michael's Church   *OS Sheet 90,
Ref NY 488264*

Location	1½ miles northeast of Pooley Bridge, Ullswater and about 4 miles southwest of Penrith — off the B5320
How to get there	From M6 Junction 40, A66, A6 over the River Eamont, B5320. The church is signposted

Facilities	Small parking area and refreshments at Pooley Bridge
Other places of interest	★Dalemain *(see p108)* on A592, northwest of the church
	★Brougham Castle, off the A66 just over 1 mile east of M6 Junction 40 *(see p115)*

 Eusemere car park, Pooley Bridge, Cumbria
☎ (085 36) 530

Brougham Castle

Brougham Castle is located on the bank of the River Eamont, just east of Penrith next to the site of the Roman fort of Brocavum. The main routes from England to Scotland and from Yorkshire to Cumberland once intersected at Brougham, and so the primary function of the castle was initially to guard this crossroad.

Medieval records of 1228 credit Robert de Vipont with the building of a keep early in the 13th century. The original castle would have comprised a stone keep, surrounded by timber outer-buildings, a ditch and a stockade. The Vipont heiress, Isabella, was married to Roger de Clifford. Their son, also called Roger, was killed in the Welsh Wars and so the legacy passed to Roger and Isabella's grandson, Robert, First Lord Clifford, in 1283. Before his death at Bannockburn in 1314, the first Lord made the keep into the nerve centre of a defensive pocket, constructing both inner and outer gate houses (c1300), each with a portcullis. He added a top floor to the castle and erected the 'Tower of League' in the southwest corner. A curtain wall may also have been built during Robert's tenure. The first Lord's grandson, another Roger, changed the layout of Brougham during his lifetime (1333-89) by adding a hall on the first floor, a chapel and a kitchen to the south.

After Roger's death the castle slowly deteriorated and it was at least 250 years before the great Clifford stalwart, Lady Anne, eventually restored the castle to its former splendour. She died at Brougham in 1676.

Interesting features at Brougham include a circular stairway which emerges on to a west-facing arcade on the castle's top floor. If this passage is followed round three sides, it leads to the entrance of a tiny octagonal room in the southeast angle. This was the Clifford's private chapel. Its vault has a central boss with eight supporting ribs.

Although today the visitor will enter the castle via the outer gatehouse to the east, a gap in the wall of the 'kitchen court' suggests that the original entrance was located on the south side.

Left:
The southwest 'Tower of League'.

Below:
Brougham Castle.

There are no windows on the north side (facing the river), but the occurrence of loopholes — just large enough to accommodate the archer's bow — emphasises the defensive aspect. This contrasts with the large windows on the east side, emphasising the residential aspect of the castle.

Left:
Firing slit or 'loophole' on the northside, top floor.
Below:
View from the castle's top floor, looking north across to the River Eamont.

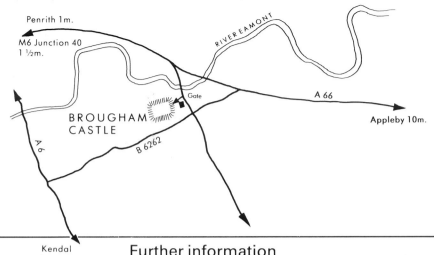

Further information

Brougham Castle   *OS Sheet 90, Ref NY 536289*
English Heritage Site

Enquiries	☎ 0768 62488
Location	1 mile east of Penrith, M6 Junction 40, off the A66 on the bank of the River Eamont. Well signposted

Admission charged

Opening times	Summer: 15 March-15 October Monday-Saturday 9.30am-6.30pm; Sunday 2pm-6.30pm Winter: 16 October-14 March Monday-Saturday 9.30am-4pm; Sunday 2pm-4pm
Facilities	🚗; refreshments at Penrith
Other places of interest	★Countess Pillar — east of the Castle on the A66 ★St Michael's Church, Barton *(see p111)*, 4 miles southwest ★Dalemain on A592, 4 miles southwest

ℹ Robinsons School, Middlegate, Penrith, Cumbria ☎ (0768) 67466

Little Salkeld Mill

Northeast of Penrith is the tiny village of Little Salkeld. The Mill, which stands on Sunnygill Beck, is one of few surviving corn mills still in operation which produces traditional stoneground flour. Mills have existed at Little Salkeld for centuries; the present Mill is in fact the third to have been built in the locality by the Atkinsons, a family whose milling connections go back a long way. The Mill's main product used to be oatmeal and it was for this that Little Salkeld Mill became famous. Oats were much easier to cultivate in the Lakeland climate and with horses to feed, oats also provided fodder.

When Britain started to import Canadian wheat, it made economic sense to build the mills at the ports. This spelled the decline of the traditional mill in the 1950s. However, during the 1970s interest in health foods began to grow and the increase in demand for such foods was one of the factors which enabled the phoenix to rise from the ashes; and so it was that early in 1975, millwright John Fairbanks, and local people restored and renewed the existing machinery to bring the Mill back to life.

Water from the beck turns two 'overshot' wheels. The larger wheel is used to drive the millstones and sack hoist. The smaller wheel powers the machinery which cleans the grain. In 1980 the smaller wheel also began to power the heatpump which is used to dry out the threshed grain. Both wheels can be seen to the rear of the mill. Nicolas Jones comments in his guide to the mill that, 'in season, trout and salmon have been known to swim up only to be knocked unconscious by the wheel, giving the miller his supper!' Dried grain (of about 12-15% moisture) is first winnowed — a cleaning process which effectively removes any bits of straw and weeds — by means of a fan. Once clean, the grain is fed into a hopper located above the stones. Once ground, the resulting product is 100% wholewheat flour. During the milling process nothing has been added or taken away. The 100% wholewheat flour produced at Little Salkeld Mill not only contains the germ, which is high in protein, but also the outer shell (the bran) which provides much needed roughage. Today the Mill can be visited by appointment.

Long Meg and Her Daughters

About one mile north of the Mill, standing amongst trees on farmland, is a huge ancient stone circle dating back to Neolithic times (c1500BC). A circumference of 1,198ft (365m) formed of 59 stones, makes the circle the largest in Cumbria and indeed one of the largest in the country. The tallest stone is Long Meg herself, nearly 18ft (5.5m) high. She bears faint 'cup and ring' markings and stands apart from, and leans in towards, the other stones — her daughters.

Many theories have been put forward over the centuries as to the use of Long Meg and similar circles, which range from the religious to the sacrificial, but nothing is clear and one can still only guess their purpose. According to legend, Long Meg was a witch who used to dance with her lovers on the Sabbath. For this sin she was turned to stone.

Although not quite as well known as Keswick's Castlerigg stone circle, Long Meg and Her Daughters is much larger and is certainly as impressive, if not more so.

Far left:
The Mill floor.

Centre left:
Ancient ring markings on Long Meg.

Left:
Long Meg and her Daughters.

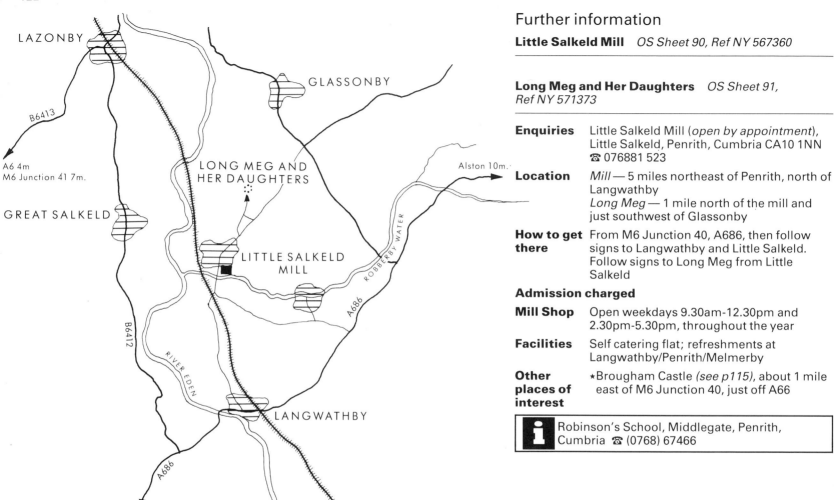

LAZONBY

B6413

A6 4m.
M6 Junction 41 7m.

GLASSONBY

GREAT SALKELD

LONG MEG AND
HER DAUGHTERS

Alston 10m.

ROBBERBY WATER

LITTLE SALKELD
MILL

A686

B6412

RIVER EDEN

LANGWATHBY

A686

Penrith 4m.
M6 Junction 40 6 M.

Further information

Little Salkeld Mill *OS Sheet 90, Ref NY 567360*

Long Meg and Her Daughters *OS Sheet 91,
Ref NY 571373*

Enquiries	Little Salkeld Mill (*open by appointment*), Little Salkeld, Penrith, Cumbria CA10 1NN ☎ 076881 523
Location	*Mill* — 5 miles northeast of Penrith, north of Langwathby *Long Meg* — 1 mile north of the mill and just southwest of Glassonby
How to get there	From M6 Junction 40, A686, then follow signs to Langwathby and Little Salkeld. Follow signs to Long Meg from Little Salkeld

Admission charged

Mill Shop	Open weekdays 9.30am-12.30pm and 2.30pm-5.30pm, throughout the year
Facilities	Self catering flat; refreshments at Langwathby/Penrith/Melmerby
Other places of interest	★Brougham Castle (*see p115*), about 1 mile east of M6 Junction 40, just off A66

Robinson's School, Middlegate, Penrith,
Cumbria ☎ (0768) 67466

Shap Abbey

The ruins of an abbey dedicated to St Mary can be seen 1½ miles west of Shap village, in a valley, on the bank of the River Lowther. Not much is known about the Abbey's history because ancient records have been lost, but we do know that this Abbey was founded in around 1180 at Preston Patrick (south of Kendal); towards the end of the 12th century the site was moved to Shap after Gospatrick's son, Thomas, had granted the land which enabled a small sanctuary to be built by 12 Premonstratensian monks, who originated from Prémontré in the north of France. The monks, called 'White Canons' because of the colour of their habits, lived a semi-sequestered life, combining solitary prayer with outside work in neighbouring homesteads.

In the aftermath of the Dissolution the monks were forced to leave this holy place, but each received a gratuity. The building itself, by now a mere shell, was left unroofed to fester.

The layout of this late 12th century Abbey can be seen today with bases of columns and parts of walls surviving at the east end, but the most interesting feature is the west tower, which was built during the early 16th century.

Below:
The early 16th century west tower.

Below left:
Remains of the east buildings.

West tower — detail.

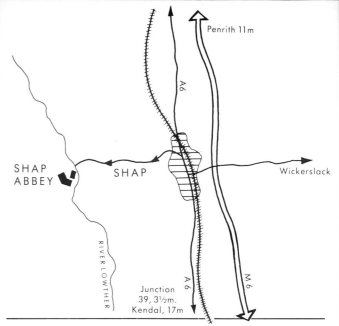

Penrith 11m

A6

SHAP ABBEY

SHAP

Wickerslack

RIVER LOWTHER

A6

M6

Junction 39, 3½m. Kendal, 17m

Further information

Shap Abbey   *OS Sheet 90, Ref NY 548153*
English Heritage Site

Location	1½ miles west of Shap Village (on A6), on the bank of the River Lowther
How to get there	From M6 Junction 39, B6261, then A6 to Shap. Turn off A6 at Shap and follow the signposts to the Abbey
Admission charge	Free
Facilities	🚗; **WC** and refreshments in Shap
Other places of interest	*Brougham Castle *(see p115),* just east of M6, Junction 40, 12 miles via A6/M6

 Robinson's School, Middlegate, Penrith, Cumbria ☎ (0768) 67466

Acknowledgements

My heartfelt thanks go to the following:

Abbot Hall and the Museum of Lakeland Life and Industry — Miss V. A. J. Slowe AMA and her staff;
St Michael's Church, Barton — the Vicar and Parochial Church Council;
Belle Isle — Mrs E. H. S. Curwen and her staff;
Brougham Castle — the resident Custodian and English Heritage;
Cartmel Priory — the Vicar and Parochial Church Council;
Dalemain — Mr and Mrs Bryce McCosh and Robert and Jane Hasell-McCosh;
Dove Cottage — Dr T. T. McCormick AMA (resident Curator) and his staff/The Wordsworth Trust;
Furness Abbey — the resident Custodian and English Heritage;
Heron Mill — Don Ainslie (resident Curator), Mrs A. A. Carruthers and The Beetham Trust;
Holker Hall — Mr and Mrs Hugh Cavendish and Mrs Carolyn Johnson (administrator) and her staff;
Leighton Hall — Mr and Mrs Richard Gillow Reynolds;
Levens Hall — Mr and Mrs C. H. Bagot and Mrs Margaret Lambert (secretary);
Little Salkeld Mill — Nicholas Jones;
Muncaster Castle — Mr and Mrs P. Gordon-Duff-Pennington;
Muncaster Mill — Peter Ellis;
Rydal Mount — Mrs Mary Henderson (née Wordsworth), and her curators Don Brookes and Liz Lane;
Sizergh Castle — Mrs T. Hornyold-Strickland and The National Trust;
Stott Park Bobbin Mill — Albert Graham and Jim Dixon, Abbot Hall and English Heritage;
Swarthmoor Hall — The Religious Society of Friends and the resident curators;
Townend — Mrs Gregg and The National Trust;
St Olaf's Church, Wasdale Head — the Vicar and Parochial Church Council;
Wordsworth House — The resident Curator and The National Trust.

Kodak — for their contribution of Kodachrome 200 Professional Film;
The National Trust and English Heritage (The Royal Commission on the Historic Monuments of England) for giving me access to their sites and allowing me to take photographs;
South Lakeland District Council;
The Lake District Special Planning Board/National Park Authority;
My sister Mrs Victoria Andrew, for checking over the script and for her help and advice;
Pat Angove — for typing the script;
Nick Hellewell ABIPP of Ivy Studios for the black and white printing;
Ted Gray, Geoff Clarke and S. Earwicker at Blackpool and Fylde College — for their help in the early stages;
Adrian Waine of Littleton, Chester — for his help with the Holker Staircase photography;
My parents, Dr and Mrs J. M. Canning — for letting me use their home in Poulton-le-Fylde, Lancashire, as my northwest base during research and photography and for their advice and support during the undertaking of *Historic Lakeland*.

In addition I would like to thank my colleague Ian G. Sellars, ABIPP, AMPA of Bromley, Kent, not only for the back cover photograph, but also for his invaluable practical advice and help during my time in London.

Special thanks must go to my good friend, Alistair E. Paxton Baines, BA (Hons), B Arch, of Knott-End-on-Sea, Blackpool, for his time and trouble in painstakingly drawing all the maps for the book — a Herculean task.

Small leaf Rhododendron.

Index